9/00

NEB

D1172607

ATHEISTS, AGNOSTICS, and DEISTS in AMERICA

ATHEISTS, AGNOSTICS, and DEISTS in AMERICA

A Brief History

Peter M. Rinaldo

DorPete Press
Briarcliff Manor, New York

Publisher's Cataloging-in-Publication
(Provided by Quality Books, Inc.)

Rinaldo, Peter M. (Peter Merritt), 1922-
        Atheists, agnostics, and Deists in America: a
    brief history / Peter M. Rinaldo, -- 1st ed.
        p.cm.
        Includes bibliographical references and index.
        LCCN: 00-131022
        ISBN: 1-890849-03-0

        1. Atheism--United States--History
    2. Agnosticism--History. 3. Deism--United States--
    History. I. Title

    BL2760.R56 2000   211.8'0973
                               QB100-311

AUTHOR'S NOTE

If one looks up the subject "Atheism - History" in the catalog of the New York Public Library, one of the world's premier research institutions, one can find books on the history of atheism in England, France, Germany, Italy, Russia, and even Lithuania. However, there is no listing for a history of atheism in the United States. This book was written to fill that gap.

Even if the New York Public does not have a book on the specific subject of the history of American atheism, their collection provides ample research material for this area. I also found the collections of the Westchester Library System libraries very helpful, and I want to thank John Hawkins of the Ossining Public Library for his assistance with numerous interlibrary loan requests.

The first draft of this book was read and reviewed by three ministers—Rev. Jay Eckman of The Presbyterian Church-New England Congregational Church in Saratoga Springs, NY; Rev. Robert W. Hare, a retired Presbyterian minister; and Rev. James Covington of the Unitarian Universalist Fellowship in Croton, NY. All of them made very helpful comments.

Finally, I would like to acknowledge and thank my wife, Dorothy Rinaldo, a retired reference librarian, for her suggestions on finding sources, as well as for her review of the many drafts of the text.

P.M.R.

CONTENTS

INTRODUCTION

This brief history examines the questions of when atheists and other nonbelievers first appeared in America; how their movement developed; and why it was never embraced by a percentage of the American people comparable to those belonging to the major religious groups.

Among the *Mayflower* Pilgrims, who landed on Plymouth Rock on November 11, 1620, there were no atheists. Nor had there been atheists in the Virginia Company that landed in Jamestown in 1607. Further, the Spanish missionaries who established garrisons and missions in Florida and the American Southwest in the early seventeenth century were Roman Catholics acting in the service of God, not denying His existence.

Nearly three hundred and eighty years after the Pilgrims landed, however, a substantial number of the inhabitants of North America were nonreligious. A 1993 Gallup Poll found that four percent of the United States population described itself as atheists or agnostics.[1] The 1999 *Statistical Abstract of the United States* lists for North America 1.6 million atheists and 27 million additional "nonreligious" inhabitants, the latter defined in a note as "persons professing no religion, nonbelievers, agnostics, freethinkers, and dereligionized secularists indifferent to all religion."[2] As part of this introduction, we shall look at definitions of atheism and the other varieties of nonbelief.

ATHEISM is simplest. The *Oxford English Dictionary* defines it as "disbelief in, or denial of, the existence of a God." It should be noted that the definition of an atheist depends upon the context of the times—which deity or deities are worshiped by the majority of the populace but whose existence is denied by the atheists. In ancient Rome, the early Christians were persecuted as atheists because they did not worship the Roman deities Jupiter and his fellow gods and goddesses. In this book, we shall use this broader sense of atheism to include all those groups in

1

America who have rejected a belief in the traditional God of the Christians, Jews, and Muslims.

DEISM was closely allied with atheism in the early days of our country. *Webster's Collegiate Dictionary* defines deism as "a movement or system of thought advocating natural religion, emphasizing morality, and in the 18th century denying the interference of the Creator with the laws of the universe." To deists, a Creator did exist, but after the creation of the universe the Creator never produced miracles, answered prayers, or otherwise interfered with natural laws. In the eighteenth and nineteenth centuries, most American Protestants and Roman Catholics considered deists to be atheists since they did not believe in the God described in the Bible nor did they subscribe to Christian tenets. The modern equivalent of a deist is a scientist such as Fred Hoyle who believes in the Big Bang theory of the origin of our universe and that a Creator was behind the Big Bang.[3] Incidentally, Hoyle is the physicist who coined the term "Big Bang."[4]

In the late twentieth century the term "deist" is popularly used interchangeably with "theist," a believer in God, although, as noted above, deism in the eighteenth and early nineteenth century was considered by Christians to be equivalent to atheism. By 1850, the use of the terms "deist" and "deism" had generally disappeared and were replaced by "freethinker" and "free thought," terms which encompassed deism, agnosticism, and atheism. As we approach the end of the twentieth century, when this book is being written, freethinker and freethought have largely dropped out of current usage, although the newspaper *Freethought Today* is still being published. Deist and deism are again being used in their proper sense, with some scientists such as Harvard biologist Edward O. Wilson again calling themselves deists.[5]

An AGNOSTIC, according to *Webster's Collegiate,* is "one who holds the view that any ultimate reality (as God) is unknown and probably unknowable." The *Oxford English Dictionary* adds

INTRODUCTION

"especially that a First Cause and an unknown world are subjects of which we know nothing." Unlike the atheists and the deists, who formed separate organized societies to meet and discuss their beliefs, agnostics have generally been independent thinkers or have remained within traditional religious sects. One can find both Roman Catholic and Protestant agnostics who consider themselves Christians.

It is interesting to note that nonbelievers have split apart into a number of different groups, depending on the degree and nature of their <u>disbelief</u> in God, just as the believers have divided into a number of sects depending on the details of their <u>beliefs</u> in God and the proper way to worship Him. Some of these sects, such as Socinianism, Arianism, and Arminianism, are no longer familiar to modern readers. Accordingly, these names and other terms are listed in the Glossary.

As we shall see in Chapter III, atheism and deism appeared in America in the eighteenth century through books by French atheists and English deists imported from Europe. Reinforcement of the views in the books was provided by European immigrants such as the English thinker Thomas Paine or by American diplomats such as Thomas Jefferson who visited Europe and heard the views of atheists and deists there. Many of the European atheists and deists, in turn, were strongly influenced by Greek philosophers such as Democritus and Epicurus, as well as Romans such as Lucretius. Greek and Latin texts by these and other philosophers were also found in the libraries of educated eighteenth-century Americans. Thus, the roots of American atheism and deism extend to classical Greece and Rome. Further, the philosophical underpinning of the beliefs of atheists and deists in the eighteenth century and even today is remarkably similar to that developed by the sages of the classical Greco-Roman period. Accordingly, in the next two chapters we shall briefly look at some of the seminal atheist and deist philosophers in the ancient world and their European successors.

The following three chapters explore the question of when

atheists and other nonbelievers first appeared on the American scene, including an examination of the early days of the new Republic and the first half of the nineteenth century, when Communitarianism and Transcendentalism flourished—and then disappeared. The next chapters review the careers of two well-known agnostics in the late nineteenth and early twentieth centuries, Robert Ingersoll and Clarence Darrow, as well as the development of organized groups including atheists, such as the Unitarians and the Ethical Culture movement.

We then shall attempt to answer the question of why, contrary to the expectations of thinkers from Jefferson to Einstein, atheism and agnosticism has never been a real threat to the major religions of Christians, Jews, and Muslims. The final chapter will speculate on the future for atheism, agnosticism, and deism in America.

CHAPTER I

ROOTS OF AMERICAN ATHEISM AND DEISM— GREECE AND ROME

As noted in the Introduction, the philosophical sources of atheism and deism in America extend back through the English and French writers of the Enlightenment to ancient Greece and Rome. Accordingly, we shall start this history with two schools of Greek philosophy—the Epicureans and the Stoics. The beliefs of the American deists of the eighteenth century such as Thomas Jefferson can be traced to the Epicureans, while Ralph Waldo Emerson and the other New England transcendentalists in the first half of the nineteenth century espoused a philosophy similar to that of the Stoics.

THE EPICUREANS

Democritus, a predecessor of Epicurus, was a contemporary of Socrates in the fifth century B.C. He was born in Abdera in Thrace, and on his father's death used his inheritance to travel. He visited Egypt, where he learned mathematics from the Egyptian priests, and journeyed to Persia, and possibly India.[1] Democritus is probably best known today for his deduction by pure reason that matter is composed of atoms in constant motion with empty space between them. The German historian Werner Jaeger wrote,[2] "His description of nature in terms of the interplay of countless atoms in empty space ruled by the power of chance

5

left no room for teleology."[a] Bertrand Russell comments, "The theory of the atomists, in fact, was more nearly that of modern science than any other theory propounded in antiquity."[3] Therefore, since the world could be adequately explained without introducing the idea of a first cause, Democritus saw no need for the pantheon of Greek gods.

Democritus then faced the question of the origin of religious beliefs, which in Greek times were nearly universal. If the gods did not exist, why did almost everyone believe in them? His answer was that religion arose as a result of man's fear and awe of the wonders of nature—such as thunder, lightning, earthquakes, and eclipses—attributing these to actions of the gods. He held that once these natural forces were explained rationally, religion would no longer be needed.[4]

An anecdote illustrating Democritus' scientific approach, as contrasted with the belief of most Greeks in their traditional gods, concerns one of his fellow citizens, who was out walking one day with no covering on his very bald head. With no warning, a turtle suddenly fell from the sky, hit him directly, and killed him. Since an eagle, a symbol of Zeus, had been seen soaring in the sky shortly before the accident, the townspeople believed that the unfortunate man was punished by Zeus. Democritus, however, gave a rational explanation: Eagles are fond of turtle meat but have a problem getting the meat from the shell. Accordingly, they take the turtles aloft and drop them from great heights on rocks, which shatter the shell. The eagle had mistaken the man's bald head for a shining rock—there was no need to invoke the gods.[5]

Democritus believed that the goal of life should be cheerfulness, which could best be achieved by avoiding violence and passion.[6] He is known as "the laughing philosopher" because of his amusement at the vain efforts of man.[7] Further, he believed

---

[a]Defined by Webster as "a doctrine explaining phenomena by final causes."

that everything in nature was subject to decay and dissolution and thus there was no life after death.[8]

Democritus lived to a very old age, probably more than 100 years. It is said that when he felt his faculties were waning, he refrained from eating to hasten his death. When, however, he had not yet died at the time of a festival, he prolonged his life by breathing the aroma of fresh bread in order not to spoil the festival for his sister by forcing her to go into mourning for him.[9] Although the story may be apocryphal, it shows the esteem in which he was held as not only a wise but also a caring man.

Epicurus, the founder of the Epicurean school of philosophy in Athens a century and a half later, was greatly influenced by Democritus. As noted above, Democritus believed that the goal of life should be cheerfulness. Epicurus considered imperturbable emotional calm to be the highest good, with intellectual pleasure superior to others. "Pleasure," he said, "is the beginning and end of the blessed life."[10]

Almost two thousand years later, Thomas Jefferson voiced a similar thought in his draft of the Declaration of Independence, in which he listed the "unalienable Rights" of all men as "Life, Liberty, and the pursuit of Happiness." He could have written "the pursuit of Wealth," or "the pursuit of Salvation," but he chose "Happiness,, which Webster defines as "a pleasurable satisfaction." We know that Jefferson was familiar with Epicurus. He wrote to his young protégé William Short in a letter dated October 31, 1819, "As you say of yourself, I too am an Epicurian."[11]

Unlike Democritus, Epicurus decided that the widespread belief in the gods must prove their existence. He held, however, that the gods did not bother with the human world but occupied themselves with their own pleasures. He regarded a belief in Providence as pure superstition. (These beliefs were close to the eighteenth-century deism of Jefferson and his fellow deists.) Since the Greek gods did not concern themselves with men, there was no reason to fear their anger or worry about punishment in an afterlife. Along with Democritus, Epicurus believed that after death the body and soul dispersed into their individual atoms, which were without sensation.[12]

Democritus and Epicurus influenced not only Jefferson but also Karl Marx. Marx was born in the Prussian town of Trier in 1818, eight years before Jefferson's death. The future author of the *Communist Manifesto* originally studied at the universities of Bonn and Berlin for a degree in law, but in 1839 decided to study for a doctorate in philosophy, choosing as his subject a comparison of the Greek philosophers Democritus and Epicurus. Marx especially admired Epicurus for his emphasis on free individual self-consciousness.[13] After receiving his doctorate, Marx continued to study religion and philosophy, concluding

> Religion is the sign of the oppressed creature, the feeling of a heartless world and the soul of soulless circumstances. It is the opium of the people....The criticism of religion is therefore the germ of the criticism of the valley of tears whose halo is religion.[14]

The atheism of Democritus and the deism of Epicurus are probably more acceptable to Americans today than the atheism of Karl Marx. The two Greek philosophers either did not believe in the existence of Zeus, Athena, and the other Olympians (Democritus) or did not believe that they influenced humans (Epicurus.) Since we also do not believe in the existence of the Greek gods outside of mythology, we can easily accept the disbelief of the Epicureans. The modern atheist's disbelief in the God of Moses and Jesus is, of course, much more difficult for most Americans to accept.

The Roman poet Lucretius, who lived in the first century B.C., was a contemporary of Julius Caesar. Although known primarily as a poet, he viewed himself as a philosopher, couching his thoughts in poetic form to attract more readers. He likened this to spreading honey on the lip of a cup to induce a child to drink bitter medicine.[15] The gap between our culture and his is shown by the unlikelihood that a poetic version of a philosophical treatise would achieve greater sales than the prose volume—with neither likely to make the best-seller lists.

Lucretius was an admirer of Epicurus. In fact, all of Epicurus' three hundred books have been lost, and it is only through a few letters and the poetry of Lucretius that we know Epicurus' philosophy. The whole of Lucretius' best-known poem, *Of the Nature of Things,* is devoted to refuting current Roman religious beliefs, particularly fear of the gods and fear of death. According to Lucretius, men fear the gods because at any time the gods may intervene to thwart them. They fear death because they believe the soul will survive death and be punished for sins committed during life.[16]

Like Democritus, Lucretius believed that the gods did not meddle in the affairs of men. In his poem *Of the Nature of Things*, Lucretius wrote,

> Nature, free at once and rid of her haughty lords, is seen to do all things spontaneously of herself without the meddling of the gods.[17]

As for death, his Book III contains twenty-nine separate proofs that the soul perishes with the body at death.[18] He was remarkably modern in many of his views, writing "You must admit that in other parts of space there are other earths and various races of men and kinds of wild beasts."[19] It was largely through Lucretius that the French *philosophes* at the end of the eighteenth century were led back to Epicurus and Democritus.[20]

THE STOICS

Zeno, the founder of Stoicism, established his school in Athens at the end of the fourth century B.C. at about the same time as Epicurus founded his school. Zeno was a Phoenician, born in Cyprus. He taught that God was not a separate being but that all man participate in the Divine through the divine spark—the *logos spermatikos*—within them. Unlike Epicurus, who emphasized happiness as the goal of life, Zeno stressed virtue. He taught that a wise man should be free of passion, submissive to natural law, and indifferent to pleasure and pain.[21]

The ideas of the Greek Stoics were transmitted to posterity primarily through two remarkable citizens of the Roman Empire, Epictetus and Marcus Aurelius—one a former slave and the other the Roman emperor. Epictetus was born in Phrygia in Asia Minor about 60 A.D., and his language was Greek. He was the son of a slave woman and was himself a slave in Rome for years. While enslaved, he attended the lectures of a Stoic philosopher, Musonius Rufus, and adopted the Stoic philosophy. When his master punished him by twisting his leg, Epicurus smiled and said calmly, "You will break it." When it was broken, he only said, "I told you so," and thereafter was a cripple. After Epictetus was freed, he became a teacher of philosophy, first in Rome and later in the city of Nicopolis in northern Greece. Although he was at the center of a school with a number of pupils, he continued to live in a small house with only a rush mat, a simple pallet bed, and an earthenware lamp. He did not write down his lectures, but they are preserved through the notes of one of his pupils, Flavius Arrian, who published them as *Discourses*.[22]

Epictetus believed in free will and the power of each man to mold his character in spite of adverse circumstances. His own personality combined personal gentleness with great moral power. Like Zeno, he taught that each person carried within himself or herself the divine spark, a portion of the deity. In the *Discourses*, he states:

> You are a superior thing; you are a portion separated from the deity; you have in yourself a certain portion of him. Why then are you ignorant of your own noble descent? Why do you not know whence you came? Will you not remember when you are eating, who you are who eat, and

whom you feed? When you are in conjunction with a woman, will you not remember who you are who do this thing? When you are in social intercourse, when you are exercising yourself, when you are engaged in discussion, know you not that you are nourishing a god, that you are exercising a god? Wretch, you are carrying about a god with you and you know it not. Do you think I mean some god of silver or of gold, and external? You carry him within yourself, and you perceive not that you are polluting him by impure thoughts and dirty deeds.[23]

A generation after Epictetus, Marcus Aurelius was born in 121 A.D. to a patrician family in Rome. At the age of eleven, Marcus became acquainted with Stoicism and decided to practice its followers' austere way of life. He so impressed the Emperor Hadrian that Hadrian advised his designated successor, Antoninus, to adopt the boy and make him his heir. Antoninus followed this advice, adopted Marcus, and betrothed him to his daughter Faustina. Marcus became co-emperor in the year 161 A.D. with the other adopted son of Antoninus, and the sole emperor in 169.

During Marcus Aurelius' reign, the Roman Empire was faced with uprisings in the Near East and along the Danube. During his campaigns to suppress the uprisings, he wrote down (in Greek) his thoughts on moral subjects as *Meditations*, apparently intending them for no eyes but his own. When the writings were found after his death, however, they were preserved and have inspired others down to the present age. The following are a few quotations:

Everything is right for me, which is right for you, O Universe. Nothing for me is too early or too late, which comes in due time for you. Everything is fruit to me which your seasons bring, O Nature. From you are all things, in you are all things, to you all things return.[24]

Think no word or deed beneath you which is in accordance with nature, and be not diverted by some people's fault-finding, nor by their words, but if a thing is good to do or say, do not consider it unworthy of you....Go straight on, following your nature and the common nature; and the way of both is one.[25]

How small a part of the boundless and unfathomable time is assigned to every man! In a moment, it is swallowed up in the eternal. And how small a part of the whole substance, and how small a part of the universal soul! And on what a small clod of the whole earth you creep! Reflecting on all this, consider nothing to be great, except to act as your nature leads you and to endure that which the common nature brings.[26]

As we shall see in Chapter V, the New England transcendentalists, such as Emerson and Thoreau, had their roots in the Stoics, rather than the Epicureans. Before we discuss the New World counterparts of these Greek and Roman philosophies, however, we shall summarize the development of atheism and deism in post-Renaissance Europe.

CHAPTER II

ROOTS OF AMERICAN ATHEISM
AND DEISM—
ENGLAND AND FRANCE

Following the fall of Rome and the rise of Christianity, there were few avowed atheists or deists until the sixteenth century. One exception was Nicolo Macchiavelli, a Florentine famous for his book *The Prince*. Although concerned primarily with how to win and hold power, the book also touched on religion in its advice to use religion as a tool to achieve power. For those who were genuinely religious, Macchiavelli was "the arch atheist, the devil who had taught men to use religion for their own ends, who had corrupted France and brought about St. Bartholomew's Day, who had taught simple Englishmen to be atheists and who, unless his works were put down or effectively combated, would be the ruin of Christendom. His name Nicolo ('Old Nick') at that time became and has ever since remained the synonym for the devil."[1] By 1579, fifty years after his death, Machiavelli's works were very popular at Cambridge University in England, and even Queen Elizabeth was charged by her enemies of being a Machiavellian.[2] A copy of *The Prince* was in Thomas Jefferson's library.[3]

From Democritus to Machiavelli, with the exception of Epictetus, the deists and atheists we have mentioned have been educated upper-class intellectuals. However, during the late sixteenth century in England, there arose a grass-roots movement of sects known as Socinianism and Unitarianism that spread in the middle and lower classes. Both Socinians and Unitarians rejected the doctrine of the Trinity. The Socinian beliefs stemmed from an Italian lay theologian named Faustus Socinius, who asserted that Jesus was more a human being than God. After being denounced by the Inquisition for his heretical doctrines,

13

ATHEISTS, AGNOSTICS, AND DEISTS IN AMERICA

Socinius moved in succession to Switzerland, Transylvania, and Poland. His writings in Poland, particularly the *Racovian Catechism* (named after its publication site of Racow), made their way to England in the seventeenth century, where they influenced the Unitarians already there.[4] Unitarianism originated in Transylvania, where John Sigismund was a Unitarian king. Although people professing the Socinian and Unitarian beliefs were not strictly atheists, their denial of the divinity of Christ led them to be considered as atheists by the British clergy. Those who failed to recant this heresy were burned at the stake. One so burned in 1579 was a plowwright named Matthew Hammond who alleged at his trial

That Christ is not God, nor the Savior of the world, but a meere man, a sinfull man, and an abhominable idoll.

That the Holy Ghoste is not God, neither that there is any such holy Ghoste.

That Baptisme is not necessarie in the churche of God.[5]

Another Unitarian, John Lewes, went to the stake in Norwich in 1583, and Peter Cole, an Ipswich tanner, met the same fate in 1587. In sixteenth-century England, both a plowwright and a tanner probably had some elementary education but certainly were not learned men. At the other end of the social spectrum, Francis Kett, a Fellow of Cambridge University, was tried and burned in 1589 for subscribing to heresies including

That Christ is only man and synfull as other men are.

That no children ought to be baptized before their full age and to know what they should believe.[6]

In spite of the burnings, Unitarianism/Socinianism continued to thrive in England both in the lower classes and also in the universities. As we shall see in the next chapter, the

ENGLISH AND FRENCH ROOTS

Unitarian beliefs spread to North America in the late eighteenth century.

During this period in England, there were also several well-known philosophers who held beliefs that bordered on atheism. Three that we shall consider here are Thomas Hobbes, who was born in 1588, Viscount Bolingbroke, born in 1678, and David Hume, born in 1711.

Hobbes was the son of an uneducated clergyman, but was brought up by an uncle after his father lost his job and abandoned his family. His uncle saw that the young Hobbes was well read in the classics, so that Hobbes translated Euripides' *Medea* from the Greek into Latin iambic poetry when he was only fourteen years old. The following year, he went to Magdalen Hall at Oxford University. Although Hobbes concluded that the university was a waste of time, his studies there led to a recommendation from the principal of Magdalen Hall to a nobleman, William Cavendish, afterwards the first Earl of Devonshire. Since Cavendish's eighteen-year-old son had married the twelve-year-old daughter of a nobleman, Hobbes' biographer comments that Cavendish senior decided his son was more in need of a tutor than a wife, and Hobbes was hired. In 1610 he and the young nobleman made the grand tour of Europe together.[7] After their return, Hobbes lived with the Cavendish family for the next eighteen years. When his patron died in 1628, Hobbes took a position as a tutor to another young man, but after three years returned to the Cavendish family, who supported him for the balance of his life. Through his patrons, Hobbes met many of the important men of his time, including Ben Johnson and Francis Bacon. He returned to Europe several times, meeting both René Descartes and Galileo Galilei. Unlike the Unitarians, Hobbes was unwilling to die for his beliefs; one of his trips to France was to escape prosecution for his writings.

Hobbes is best known for his book *Leviathan*. In it, Hobbes argued for the need in government of a strong central authority. Without government, the life of a man in a "state of nature" is "solitary, poor, nasty, brutish, and short."[8] To counter this anarchy, Hobbes proposed that the populace should agree to a strong central government such as an absolute monarchy.[9]

Although this political side of *Leviathan* is most remembered, more than half of the book deals with religious matters. Hobbes was strongly anti-Catholic, referring to the Pope as "King of the Fairies."[10] All Hobbes' works were placed on the Vatican's *Index Librorum Prohibitorum* and remain prohibited today. In 1652, Sir Edward Nichols, a royalist, wrote of Hobbes as "that father of atheists" who "hath rendered all of the queen's court and many of the Duke of York's family atheists."[11] In his writing, however, Hobbes was a deist, not an atheist. Since he was knowledgeable in Greek and Latin (as shown by his translation of *Medea* from Greek to Latin), he may have been familiar with the philosophies of Epicurus and Lucretius. If not, he independently reached the same conclusion as Lucretius—that the universe had been set in motion by a first cause, which could be regarded as God. Hobbes did not, however, believe in a personal God or in the Bible's version of history.[12]

Hobbes' philosophy that a strong central government is required to prevent anarchy has never been widely accepted. Nevertheless, the late twentieth-century experiences with anarchy in Somalia and Rwanda show that, to a degree, he had a valid point of view. As for his religious beliefs, Hobbes' deism helped preserve the philosophy of deism for its eventual crossing of the ocean to America.

Henry St. John, who became Viscount Bolingbroke and is known by that name, was born in 1678, one year before Hobbes died. Although not as well known today as either Hobbes or Hume, Bolingbroke in his day was important both in politics and as a religious skeptic. He entered Parliament as a Tory shortly before the accession of Queen Anne in 1702. Two years later he was appointed Secretary for War. He became a favorite of Queen Anne and in 1710 was appointed Secretary of State and rose to become the leading figure in the government. Unfortunately for him, Queen Anne died suddenly in 1714, and her successor, William I, favored the opposition party, the Whigs. Bolingbroke was impeached for political crimes and fled to France to escape trial.

In France, he eventually bought a small estate, which he named La Source. His abrupt political change of fortune apparently led him to consider the meaning of life, and at age forty he began the study of philosophy and religion. In 1722 he received an extended visit at La Source from Voltaire, "who was much attracted to the eminent Englishman, complimented lavishly his learning, his French, his politeness, his vast reading."[13] Whether Voltaire primarily influenced Bolingbroke or vice versa is a moot question. Voltaire frequently praised Bolingbroke and in part admitted his debt to him.

In 1723 Bolingbroke was allowed to return to England, where he purchased an estate called Dawley Farm near the estate of Alexander Pope, the greatest English poet of the time. The two men "undoubtedly engaged in countless philosophical discussions, Pope always looking to Bolingbroke as his tutor and guide."[14] It is likely that Bolingbroke influenced Pope's major work, *Essay on Man*. In 1726 Bolingbroke's old friend Voltaire was exiled to England for two years for his religious views and spent part of the time at Dawley Farm. In the following years, Bolingbroke wrote articles for the opposition political journal *The Craftsman*, but he never regained political influence. During his later life, he alternated his residence between England and France.

Bolingbroke's philosophical and religious writings were not published until after his death in 1751. These primarily expounded his religious beliefs. He professed belief in God but rejected the remainder of Christianity, espousing what he called "natural religion," which he said was discoverable by every rational man, rather than being revealed by a higher authority. Science, through its observation and analysis, helps man find "the true religion, the religion of nature."[15] According to one of his biographers, "He laughed at the Old Testament as a farrago of nonsense and lies."[16] He also termed Saint Paul a fanatical visionary.[17]

Bolingbroke's posthumously published *Works* were immediately attacked by the religiously orthodox. James Boswell, biographer of Dr. Samuel Johnson, recorded Johnson as saying, "[Bolingbroke] was a scoundrel for charging a blunderbuss against religion and morality."[18] On the other hand, Bolingbroke's influence on the thinking of Voltaire, Pope, and Hume assured his immortality. Finally, as will be seen in the next chapter, of the European deistic philosophers, it was Bolingbroke who most influenced Thomas Jefferson.

The historian Herbert Marais writes

> The publication of Lord Bolingbroke's essays (1752-4) marked the peak of the deistic movement in England. Up to the middle of the eighteenth century, deism had spread widely among rich and poor, learned and unlearned. About 1750, an orthodox German traveler, citing the *British Magazine,* stated that half of the educated people in England were deists. Some twenty years before, a proclamation by the college heads of Oxford lamented the progress of deism among the student body.[19]

The third British philosopher whom we shall consider is David Hume. Born in Edinburgh in 1711, Hume entered the University of Edinburgh at the age of twelve but left three years later without a degree. Shortly thereafter, he lost all his religious faith. His most important work, *Treatise of Human Nature,* was written while he was living in France. In spite of abandoning religious faith, he managed to establish good relations with the priests of a Jesuit college with an excellent library, which he used for research on his *Treatise.*[20] In the book, Hume agrees with the philosopher John Locke that all ideas are ultimately derived from experience through impressions. He wrote that man is "nothing but a heap or collection of different perceptions, which succeed each other with an inconceivable rapidity, and are in a perpetual flux and movement."[21]

Hume was not sympathetic to conventional religion. In his essay "Of Miracles," he stated

> There is not to be found in all history any miracle attested by a sufficient number of men of such unquestioned good sense,

education, and learning, as to secure us against all delusion in themselves, of such undoubted integrity as to place them beyond all suspicion of any design to deceive others... [22]

Hume did not believe in life after death. Nor did he believe in a personal God accessible by prayer, intervening in human affairs, and worthy of adoration.[23] Hume specifically attempted to refute three of the principal arguments made by philosophers and theologians for the existence of God:

1. Every finite thing has a cause, which in turn has a cause. Since this series cannot be infinite, there has to be a first cause, the uncaused cause of everything. This first cause is obviously God. This reasoning is also known as the *a priori* argument.. Hume answers:

In tracing an eternal succession of objects, it seems absurd to enquire for a general cause or first author. How can anything that exists from eternity have a cause, since that relation implies a priority in time and a beginning of existence?

In such a chain, too, or succession of objects, each part is caused by that which preceded it, and causes that which succeeds it. Where then is the difficulty? But the *whole*, you say, wants a cause. I answer that the uniting of these parts into a whole, like the uniting of several distinct countries into one kingdom, or several distinct members into one body, is performed by an arbitrary act of the mind, and has no influence on the nature of things. Did I show you the particular cause of each individual in a collection of twenty particles of matter, I would think it very unreasonable should you afterwards ask me the cause of the whole twenty. This is sufficiently explained in explaining the cause of the parts.

The argument *a priori* has seldom been found very convincing, except to people of a metaphysical head, who have accustomed themselves to abstract reasoning, and who finding from mathematics that the understanding frequently leads to truth, through obscurity, and contrary to first appearances, have transferred the same habit of thinking to subjects where it ought not to have a place. Other people, even of good sense and the best inclined to religion, feel always some deficiency in such arguments, though they are not perhaps able to explain distinctly where it lies. A certain proof that men ever did, and ever will, derive their religion from other sources than from this species of reasoning.[24]

2. The second argument is known as the ontological argument, which was invented by Saint Anselm and endorsed by Descartes. This depends on the distinction between existence and essence. An imaginary person or thing can have essence, such as color or personality, but may not in reality exist. In the case of God, however, Saint Anselm and Descartes maintain that essence does imply existence because God, who is perfect in all respects, would not be perfect if He did not exist.

Hume's reply is:

The idea of existence is nothing different from the idea of any object, and that when after the simple conception of anything we would conceive it as existent, we in reality make no addition or alteration to our first idea. But I go farther; and not content with asserting that the conception of the existence of any object is no addition to the simple conception of it, I likewise maintain that the belief of existence joins no new ideas to those, which compose the idea of the object.[25]

3. The argument from design contends that many things in the world cannot plausibly be explained as the product of blind natural forces. The only reasonable explanation is that they must have been created by a beneficent God.

Hume's reply is that the adaptation of organisms to their purposes may not have resulted from the design by God but by nature's slow and bungling experiments through thousands of years (thus anticipating Darwin by 100 years). He goes on to say:

Look around this universe. What an immense profusion of beings, animated and organized, sensible and active! You admire this prodigious variety and fecundity. But inspect a little more narrowly these living existences....How hostile and destructive to each other!...The whole presents nothing but the idea of a blind nature, impregnated by a great vivifying principle, and pouring forth from her lap, without discernment or parental care, her maimed and abortive children.[26]

These beliefs naturally brought him into conflict with the Church of Scotland, and he was charged with heresy. He was, however, defended by friends among the moderate clergy on the grounds that a nonbeliever lay outside the jurisdiction of the Church.[27] In spite of his rejection of organized religion, Hume was not a complete atheist. In fact on one of his visits to France, Hume expressed to his host, Baron d'Holbach, his doubt of the actual existence of atheists. The Baron assured him, "Here you are at table with seventeen."[28] One of his biographers characterizes Hume's beliefs as "a highly attenuated deism, which is not positively advocated."[29] Hume admitted the theoretical possibility of the universe having had an intelligent origin but denied that there was any subsequent participation by a Creator in His creation.

Hume was much admired by Thomas Jefferson, who while he was in Paris sent two trunks of books to James Madison, including the collected works of Hume. These Madison studied in preparation for the Constitutional Convention.[30]

At Hume's burial in 1776, a voice in the crowd proclaimed, "He was an atheist," and was answered by another voice remarking, "No matter, he was an honest man."[31] Reportedly, the crowd remained all night hoping to see the Devil come to claim Hume's soul.

Among those influenced by Bolingbroke and Hume were two distinguished French philosophers, Voltaire and Denis Diderot. Voltaire referred to Hume as "My St. David." Diderot wrote to Hume, "I salute you, I love you, I revere you."[32] Because Hume, Diderot, and Voltaire all influenced such prominent Americans as Thomas Jefferson and James Madison, we shall continue this chapter by considering the lives and religious philosophies of Voltaire and Diderot.

Voltaire was born in 1694, nineteen years before Diderot. Originally named François-Marie Arouet, he changed his name to Voltaire in 1718. "Voltaire" is thought to be a rough anagram of Arouet

L.J., short for Arouet Le Jeune, with the 'u' changed to a 'v' and the 'j' to an 'I'. At the age of nine, young François-Marie was sent as a boarder to the Jesuit College Louis-Le-Grand in Paris, where he remained for seven years studying the classics, French literature, and history. Although his father wished him to become a lawyer, François-Marie decided on a career as a writer. His father disapproved of this decision and arranged to have him sent as an attaché to the French embassy in The Hague. However, an affair with the daughter of a French Huguenot in the Hague led to his recall to Paris. His father was so angry that he threatened to send him to the West Indies, but François-Marie placated him by consenting to enter a law office. He lasted no longer in the law office than he had in the embassy, but found refuge in the country house of a family friend, where he composed a tragedy in verse, *Oedipe*. He returned to Paris in 1716, where he continued to write verse. One of the poems implied that the Regent for Louis XV was committing incest with his daughter, the Duchess of Berry. This and other poems eventually caused the Regent to sentence François-Marie to the Bastille, where he remained for eleven months. Prison conditions were not onerous, and he was allowed books and visitors, and time to write. He composed a long history in verse about Henri de Navarre, titled *Le Hanriade*. After his release from the Bastille (and change of name to Voltaire), his earlier play *Oedipe* was produced with great success, leading to a pension from the Regent. This pension, combined with an inheritance from his father and successful investments, resulted in Voltaire becoming financially independent.[33]

Throughout his long life, Voltaire was engaged in controversy. He hated injustice, tyranny, and narrowness of mind and was not afraid to incorporate his views in his plays and books. Consequently, his books were continually being burned, and Voltaire was threatened with imprisonment. He was sent back to the Bastille in 1726 but was released when he agreed to go into voluntary exile in England. There he stayed with Bolingbroke part of the time and met some of the leading English deists. He paid the fine for one, Thomas Woolston, who had been imprisoned for his beliefs[34]. In 1729 he returned to France, impressed with the freedom of the English people in comparison with that of the French.

ENGLISH AND FRENCH ROOTS

Voltaire's most famous work is *Candide, ou l'optimisme*, published in 1759. The hero, Candide, was the bastard son of a nobleman's sister "by a good and honorable gentleman of the neighborhood whom that demoiselle refused to marry." Candide is tutored by Professor Pangloss who could prove that "in this best of all possible worlds, the Baron's castle was the most magnificent of all castles and Milady the best of all possible Baronesses (despite her 350 pounds)." The book describes a series of adventures of Candide and his beloved, Cunégonde, the nobleman's daughter. Voltaire in the story manages to satirize "religious abuses, class prejudices, political corruption, legal chicanery, judicial venality...the injustice of slavery, and the destructiveness of war."[35]

Benjamin Franklin, who performed various diplomatic missions for the United States in France between 1776 and 1793, knew and respected Voltaire. The historian Joseph J. Ellis writes:

> When Franklin and Voltaire embraced before the multitudes of Paris, it created a sensation in the French press, the union of the two greatest champions of human enlightenment in history's most enlightened century.[36]

Years later, Franklin took his fifteen-year-old grandson to visit Voltaire, who blessed the boy, saying in English, "God and Liberty."[37]

Throughout his career, Voltaire attacked the Catholic Church. In his personal beliefs, he rejected supernatural doctrines and all religious creeds. As Norman Torres explains in *The Spirit of Voltaire,* writes

> Voltaire believed in the existence of an intelligent supreme being who was responsible for the unchanging laws of the universe. Having created and ordered the world from matter, he gave it a tap to set it in motion, and his job was done.[38]

This is essentially the deistic position, although Voltaire often referred to himself as a theist. He once wrote, "If God did not exist, it would be necessary to invent him."[39] In any case, Voltaire was an atheist only in the sense that he did not believe in the God of the Christians and

Jews. In this he differed from his friend and colleague Diderot, who was a thoroughgoing atheist.

Denis Diderot, born in 1713, was nineteen years younger than Voltaire, but followed a similar path of initially considering the priesthood, switching to law, and eventually making a career as an author and editor. Diderot attended a Jesuit school in the town of his birth, Langes, from his eighth to his fifteenth year. He was given the Jesuit's shaven crown at age twelve, wore a black cassock, and resolved to become a Jesuit priest. He later explained that he had mistaken "the first stimuli of a developing sexuality for the voice of God."[40] He continued his education for a time at the Jesuit College Louis-Le-Grand in Paris, the same college which Voltaire had attended. He eventually dropped his aspirations to become a priest and supported himself by becoming a lawyer's apprentice. Continuing his studies of Latin and Greek, Diderot was especially drawn to Democritus, Epicurus, and Lucretius.[41] His biographer P.N. Furbank states that the most important influence on Diderot's philosophic thinking was

> The grand materialistic world-view of Lucretius in *De rerum natura*. That the senses are the foundation of all belief and the only source of knowledge; that there is a plurality of worlds and an infinite universe; that there are no "final causes"; that the Gods, if Gods there be, take no interest in mankind; and that the chief goods of human existence are a body free of pain and a mind not enslaved by superstitious fear.[42]

In 1746, Diderot anonymously issued a small book, *Pensées philosophiques,* which rejected Christianity in favor of "natural religion" (the equivalent of deism) and denounced the Catholic Church for its intolerance and persecution.[43] He himself was soon a victim of this persecution, for his religious views became known and he was imprisoned in a solitary cell in the castle of Vincennes. Eventually friends and family arranged for his release.

Diderot is best known as the editor of the *Encyclopédie,* a large work that sought to gather all known knowledge of the arts and sciences in a popular form. He recruited experts in their fields to write on their

24

specialties, and eventually the work ran to seventeen volumes of text, plus eighteen volumes of plates. Voltaire, who was then living in Switzerland, contributed articles on Elegance, Eloquence, and Intelligence, as well as a learned article on Fornication. Diderot wrote many of the articles himself, including those on Epicurus and Hobbes, as well as entries on boa constrictors, playing cards, stockings, and breweries.[44] For an expensive and erudite work, it was very popular. The volumes were reprinted in Switzerland, Italy, Germany, and Russia, and study groups similar to our Great Books groups were formed to read and discuss it. Thomas Jefferson advised James Madison to buy it.[45]

Like Voltaire, Diderot enjoyed financial support from outside sources to supplement his income from his books. In Diderot's case, Empress Catherine the Great, of Russia, became his benefactor. In 1765 Diderot's friend Friedrich Grimm learned that the writer had decided to sell his library to raise funds for his daughter's dowry. Grimm, who knew Empress Catherine, proposed to her that she buy the library. She not only agreed but suggested that the library remain on deposit in Diderot's house and that he be paid a salary of one hundred *pistoles* a year as her librarian.[46] Subsequently he visited Russia at Catherine's request and tried unsuccessfully to persuade her to reorganize her empire along democratic lines.

At the time he wrote *Pensées philosophic* in 1746, Diderot was a deist, persuaded that a deity existed by the "argument from design"; that is, the complexity of natural life shows conclusively the existence of an intelligent designer, God. By the time Diderot completed the *Encyclopédie*, however, he was an outright atheist, writing "I would sacrifice my life, perhaps, if I could annihilate forever the notion of God." He also wrote that "Of all religions, Christianity is the most absurd and the most atrocious in its dogma."[47] Nevertheless, he concealed these radical opinions in order to escape another prison sentence and so that he could continue to publish his works.

Diderot felt that one could both be an atheist and a moral person. In *The Nephew of Rameau,* written in 1761 but not published until after his death, Diderot explained:

I do not condemn the pleasure of the senses. I too have a palate that relishes delicate dishes and delicious wines. But—I will not conceal it from you—it seems to me infinitely sweeter to have helped the unfortunate...to have given salutary counsel, to have read an agreeable book, to take a walk with a man or woman dear to me, to have given some instructive hours to my children, to have written a good page, to fulfill the duties of my place...[48]

Although Diderot did not always live up to this creed, he was much admired by contemporaries and successors. Jean-Jacques Rousseau wrote of him, " At the distance of several centuries Diderot will seem a prodigious man. People will look from afar at that universal head with mingled admiration and astonishment, as we look today at the heads of Plato and Aristotle."[49]

None of the European philosophers we have discussed in this chapter—Thomas Hobbes, Viscount Bolingbroke, David Hume, Voltaire, and Denis Diderot—traveled to the New World. Their ideas freely crossed the Atlantic, however, transported in books and in the minds of those Americans who had been exposed to their philosophies while sojourning in England and France. Among these Americans were men often considered the Founding Fathers of the new Republic, including Benjamin Franklin, Thomas Jefferson, James Madison, and John Adams. In the next chapter, we shall examine the degree to which their reading and their contacts in Europe influenced the religious views of these eminent men. We shall also review the lives and religious beliefs of two of their influential immigrant contemporaries—Thomas Paine, and Joseph Priestly.

CHAPTER III

ATHEISM AND DEISM IN THE NEW REPUBLIC

Although none of the Founding Fathers of the United States were atheists, many were accused of being so because they were not members of one of the Protestant churches or because they expressed unorthodox beliefs. As late as 1830, the Philadelphia Public Library refused to place any of Thomas Jefferson's writings on its shelves, calling him an infidel.[1]

Although not atheists, some of the Founding Fathers were deists, which the reader may recall is the term used in the eighteenth and nineteenth centuries to describe those who believed in a Creator but denied that the Creator thereafter ever interfered with the natural laws of the universe, such as producing miracles or answering prayers. We shall commence our history of atheism and deism in the new Republic by reviewing the lives and religious beliefs of four of the Founding Fathers—Benjamin Franklin, Thomas Jefferson, John Adams, and James Madison—as well as two influential immigrants, Thomas Paine and Joseph Priestley. Jefferson and Adams were atheists only in the broad sense that they rejected the beliefs of most of their fellow Americans in a God who did answer prayers and produce miracles. Franklin was a deist in his youth and seems to have continued to hold deistic beliefs as an adult, although he also maintained a loose association with the Presbyterian church. Adams, too, was a deist in his youth and a nonconforming freethinker later in his life. As an adult Jefferson termed himself both a deist and a Unitarian, although he never joined the Unitarian church. In his mature years, Madison also expressed a preference for Unitarianism, without becoming a member of any church. All of these men (with the exception of Madison, who did not travel abroad) were influenced by the three routes mentioned in the last chapter whereby heretical ideas reached American shores—through books written by Europeans, through association with European immigrants with unorthodox religious beliefs, and through their travels in Europe, which exposed them to controversial religious thinkers.

We shall start with Thomas Jefferson, born in Albemarle County, Virginia in 1743. In many cases, our religious beliefs as adults are similar to those of our parents and thus reflect our early education both at home and at the Sunday schools of the churches that our parents attended. This was not true with Jefferson, whose parents were members of the Church of England (known as Episcopalian following the American Revolution.) He was educated at home along with his sisters and cousins by a tutor hired by his father to teach the children in a one-room schoolhouse on the grounds of their estate. According to one of his biographers, "He had religion drummed into him by his tutor" and "He had to learn his prayers by rote as if they were sums."[2] When he was nine years old, he was sent during the week to study with the Reverend William Douglas, who taught him elementary Latin and Greek, as well as how to speak French with a Scottish accent. At age fifteen, after his father's death, he transferred to a small academy operated by the Reverend James Maury, a graduate of the College of William and Mary, in Williamsburg, Virginia. Maury had later traveled to England to be ordained in the Church of England.[3] It is unlikely that Jefferson's deistic beliefs as an adult stemmed either from his childhood upbringing or from the Reverends Douglas and Maury.

In March 1760, just before he reached age seventeen, Jefferson set off for the College of William and Mary, whose faculty at that time numbered only seven, of whom all but one were Anglican clergymen. Fortunately, that one layman, Dr. William Small, took Jefferson under his wing. Jefferson later wrote:

> Dr. William Small of Scotland was the professor of Mathematics, a man profound in most of the useful branches of

Science, with a happy talent of communication, correct and gentlemanly manners, and an enlarged and liberal mind. He, most happily for me, became soon attached to me and made me his daily companion when not engaged in school; and from his conversation I got my first views of the expansion of science and of the system of things in which we are placed.[4]

Small had come to William and Mary in 1758, two years before Jefferson, and taught not only mathematics but also ethical philosophy. He was a product of the Scottish Enlightenment, in which "Scotland's five universities had far outdistanced Oxford and Cambridge in the study of science, philosophy, and law."[5] Small introduced into William and Mary the philosophical skepticism of the European Enlightenment. From him, Jefferson first learned of Voltaire, Diderot, and other French thinkers.[6].

We know less about Jefferson in these early years than in his later life because a fire in his family home in 1770 destroyed his library, notes, and law records. Two years later, however, at the same time he was replacing his own lost library, he drew up for Robert Skipworth, a young friend, a list of books recommended for a basic library. The list includes four volumes of David Hume's essays, five volumes of political works by Viscount Bolingbroke, and a set of volumes by Voltaire,[7]

We noted in the last chapter that one of the ways that the deistic and atheistic ideas of European philosophers reached America was through their books. We have ample evidence of this in Jefferson's case. We not only have his 1770 list of desirable books drawn up for Skipworth but also a complete inventory of Jefferson's eventual library. The latter list was compiled in 1814 when Jefferson sold his nearly 6,500 books to the Library of Congress to replace those lost at the time that the British burned the library during the War of 1812. The inventory includes works by Lucretius, Hobbes, Bolingbroke, Hume, Voltaire, and Diderot. Of these, the writings of Lucretius and Bolingbroke appear to have been most influential.

Jefferson's library included eight different editions of poetry by Lucretius.[8] The reader will recall from the previous chapter that it is through the works of the Roman poet Lucretius that the philosophy of Epicurus, the Greek thinker who lived two hundred years earlier, was preserved. The extent of Epicurus' influence on Jefferson is shown in a letter written some years later to William Short, referred to in the previous chapter. Short was a young friend of Jefferson to whom Jefferson often referred as his foster son and who accompanied Jefferson to Paris as his secretary.

> As you say of yourself, I too am an Epicurean. I consider the genuine (not the imputed) doctrines of Epicurus as containing everything rational in moral philosophy which Greece and Rome have left us....I will place under this a syllabus of the doctrines of Epicurus, somewhat in a lapidary style, which I wrote some twenty years ago.
>
> *Syllabus of the doctrines of Epicurus*
> *Physical*—The Universe eternal.
> Its parts great and small, interchangeable.
> Matter and Void alone....
> Gods, an order of being next superior to man, enjoying in their sphere, their own felicities; but not meddling with the concerns of the scale of beings below them.
> *Moral*—Happiness is the aim of life.
> Virtue the foundation of happiness.
> Utility the test of virtue.
> Pleasure active and In-do-lent.
> In-do-lence is the absence of pain, the true felicity.[9]

As for Bolingbroke, Jefferson's library included all five volumes of his posthumously published philosophical works. Jefferson's biographer William Sterns Randall writes that Jefferson copied some ten thousand words of Bolingbroke in his

Literary Commonplace Book, six times more than those of any other author. Randall states:

> He was to a remarkable extent to adopt Bolingbroke's philosophical views: his thoroughgoing materialism, his rationalistic rejection of metaphysics and of all speculation that went beyond the human mind, his uncompromising belief in reason as the sole and final arbiter of knowledge and worth. He also absorbed Bolingbroke's opinion of churchmen as corrupters of Christianity, and he came away with a strong skepticism about the historical accuracy of the Bible.[10]

Although Jefferson's library shows the strong influence of Epicurus and Bolingbroke, it also included volumes of the Stoic philosophers Epictetus and Marcus Aurelius Antoninus. These Stoics also appear on the list mentioned above of books recommended by Jefferson to his young friend Robert Skipworth.

Jefferson, although a deist, also had a strong interest in the Bible and Christianity. His library reflects these interests. He had two copies in Greek of the Septuagint, the early translation of the Old Testament from Hebrew to Greek, as well as ten copies of the Latin Vulgate version of the whole Bible, and the complete Apocrypha. Also in Jefferson's library were the *Confessions of St. Augustine* and Thomas à Kempis' *Imitations of Christ.*[11]

In April 1762, Jefferson left William and Mary and, at the suggestion of Small, entered the law office of George Wythe, who was one of the leading trial lawyers of Virginia and a champion of religious liberties before such views became fashionable. Among Wythe's other law students over the years were John Marshall, the fourth Chief Justice of the United States Supreme Court, and James Monroe, the fifth President. Wythe also was a member of Virginia's colonial legislature, the House of Burgesses, and was thus acquainted with the leading Virginia politicians. Jefferson continued his study of law under Wythe's guidance for the next five years.[12]

In 1768 Jefferson was elected to Virginia's House of Burgesses, one of three candidates for the two seats to which Albemarle County was entitled. The Burgesses met in May 1769, but after only ten days the British-appointed governor dissolved the session on the basis that the legislature had passed resolutions declaring they had sole taxation rights and protesting removal of accused persons to England for trial. A new election was held in September 1769, and Jefferson was reelected.[13]

When the committee of correspondence was formed in 1772 to coordinate Virginia's actions against England with the other colonies, Jefferson was a founding member. In 1774 Jefferson wrote a twenty-three page pamphlet titled *A Summary View of the Rights of British America* which, while published anonymously, was widely known to be written by him. The following year Jefferson served as a member of the Virginia delegation to the Second Continental Congress and helped draft a "Declaration of the Causes and Necessity of Taking up Arms," as well as drafting a reply to a conciliatory proposal by Lord North, the official in London responsible for the colonies.[14] Jefferson's skill in writing these two documents was undoubtedly the major factor in his appointment on June 11, 1776, to the committee formed by the Continental Congress to draft the Declaration of Independence. The committee consisted of John Adams, Benjamin Franklin, Roger Sherman, Robert Livingston, and Jefferson, but it was Jefferson and Adams who were subsequently selected to do the actual writing of the draft. Adams convinced Jefferson to write the first draft, which he then submitted to Franklin and Adams, who made minor changes. Subsequent alterations of the draft by Congress were more substantial, but on July 4, 1776, the Declaration was adopted by Congress.[15]

The Declaration of Independence is recognized as Jefferson's greatest achievement. As we noted in the first chapter, the inclusion of the phrase 'pursuit of happiness" as one of the "unalienable rights" shows a debt to the Greek philosopher Epicurus, who believed pleasure to be the ultimate good and whose deistic views were similar to Jefferson's. The phrases in the Declaration "to assume among the powers of the earth the separate & equal station to which the laws of nature and nature's god entitle them" and "they are endowed by their creator with certain unalienable rights" are also more likely to have been written by a deist than by a conventional Christian. The latter probably would have substituted "Almighty God" for "nature's god" and "their creator."

This is an appropriate place to discuss the lives and religious views of Jefferson's fellow members of the committee responsible for the Declaration, John Adams and Benjamin Franklin. Adams became Vice President under President George Washington and then President from 1796 to 1800. Franklin, although he never held national political office, was one of the most influential figures in the American Revolution and at the later Constitutional convention.

Franklin was much older than Jefferson and Adams. He was born in Boston in 1706, the second youngest of seventeen children. His father originally intended for him to become a minister "as the tithe of his sons"[16] and sent him to grammar school at age eight. When Franklin was ten, however, his father took him out of school to assist him in his craft of candle maker. A year later, the boy was apprenticed to his brother James, who had learned the printing trade in England and had returned to Boston with a printing press and type. Ben and his brother eventually quarreled and Ben decided to leave Boston, partly because "my indiscrete disputations about religion began to make me pointed at with horror by good people as an infidel or atheist."[17] At another point in his *Autobiography* Franklin stated:

My parents had early given me religious impressions and brought me through childhood piously in the Dissenting

[Presbyterian] way. But I was scarce fifteen, when, after doubting by turns of several points, as I found them disputed in the different books that I had read, I began to doubt of Revelation itself. Some books against Deism fell into my hands....It happened that they wrought an effect in me quite contrary to what was intended by them; for the arguments of the Deists, which were quoted to be refuted, appeared to me much stronger than the refutations. I soon became a thorough Deist.[18]

Franklin soon returned, however, at least publicly, to more conventional beliefs. A few pages later he wrote:

Although I early absented myself from public assemblies of the sect [Presbyterian], Sunday being my studying day, I never was without some religious principles. I never doubted, for instance, the existence of the Deity; that he made the world and governed it by his providence; that the most acceptable service of God was the doing good to man; that our souls are immortal; and that all crime will be punished and virtue rewarded, either here or hereafter.... Tho' I seldom attended any public worship, I had still an opinion of its propriety, and of its utility when rightly conducted, and I regularly paid my annual subscription for the support of the only Presbyterian minister or meeting we had in Philadelphia.[19]

In Philadelphia, Franklin found employment as a journeyman printer in 1723. Advancing rapidly in the printing trade, in 1729 he purchased the newspaper *Pennsylvania Gazette* from his former boss. During the next decade, it became the most widely read newspaper in the colonies. The following year he was named official printer for Pennsylvania and in 1732 published the first *Poor Richard's Almanack,* which he continued annually. During the same period, Franklin initiated the establishment of a subscription library in Philadelphia.

The previous year, 1731, Franklin had joined the Freemasons and in 1734 became grand master of St. John's lodge in Philadelphia, the earliest Masonic lodge in America. His biographer Carl Van Doren notes that, "Freemasonry, secret, sociable, and unified, was more congenial than churches to Franklin."[20] Freemasonry is a secret order that may date back to the Middle Ages. The order emphasizes the member's duties to his family, his God, and his country. Like many secret societies, the Masons have passwords, hand grips, and a set of rituals. Their rituals refer to God as "the Great Architect" and urge members to comply with "the essentials of religion" rather than Christianity, thus giving members an opportunity to embrace deism.[21] During the balance of his life, Franklin continued his association with the Masons both in Philadelphia and abroad.(He was so highly esteemed by the Masons in France that during his residence in Paris following the Revolution, the Masonic Lodge of the Nine Sisters in Paris chose him as their grand master, *Vénérable,* in 1779.[22])

During the decades of the 1730s and 1740s, Franklin became an increasingly important public figure. He was appointed clerk of the Pennsylvania Assembly in 1736, postmaster of Philadelphia in 1737, and he founded the American Philosophical Society in 1743. During the same years he invented the Franklin stove (an efficient heating device resembling a portable fireplace widely used in nineteenth-century America) and began his experiments on the electrical nature of lightning.

In 1757 Franklin was sent by the Pennsylvania Assembly to England to negotiate the settlement of a dispute between the Pennsylvania governor, representing the Crown, and the Pennsylvania Assembly, over taxation of land of the "proprietors," the descendants of the original settlers. He remained in England for five years, successfully negotiated a settlement of the taxation matter, and became acquainted with many of the leading philosophers and scientists of England and Scotland, including David Hume, at whose home he stayed while in Edinburgh.[23] He was given honorary doctor of laws degrees by the University of St. Andrews in 1759 and Oxford University in 1762, thereafter being known as Dr. Franklin. Although he returned to Pennsylvania that same year for a two years stay, he was sent back to England by the Pennsylvania Assembly in 1764. During this stay, Franklin was instrumental in securing repeal of the hated Stamp Act, which the colonists considered "taxation without representation."

During this second English stay, Franklin also met two men whose emigration from England to America later became influential in bringing deism to the new world—Thomas Paine and Joseph Priestley. In 1774 Franklin wrote a letter of introduction to his son-in-law for "Mr. Thomas Paine...very well recommended to me as an ingenious, worthy young man....I request you give him your best advice and countenance, as he is quite a stranger there."[24] Franklin later wrote to Paine, "I value myself on the share I had in procuring for [America] the acquisition of so useful and valuable a citizen."[25]

Thomas Paine was born in Thetford, England, in 1737 to a very poor family. He eventually escaped Thetford by signing on as a sailor with a privateer, but he deserted the ship in London, whence he apprenticed himself to a maker of corset stays. He tried several other jobs, including that of tax collector, and somehow managed to save sufficient money to pay for his passage to America. He then boldly approached Franklin, who gave him the requested letters of introduction mentioned above.[26]

Although Paine was virtually unknown in England, "no man's words had a greater impact on the people of the American colonies in arousing them to the call of national independence....The open, concerted movement for national independence dates from the publication of Paine's *Common Sense* in January 1776"[27] This little pamphlet, from which Paine received no income, was published in Philadelphia, where he was then a journalist. Paine presented the first copy to his patron, Franklin.

ATHEISM AND DEISM IN THE NEW REPUBLIC

Paine's biographer John Keane wrote:

> The pamphlet was scurrilous, abusive, seditious, and
> written with an enormous sparkle; it also cunningly
> nurtured the anti-Catholic language of the Protestant
> Dissent, with the intention of making readers feel in their
> hearts that British power in the American colonies
> amounted to an *ancien regime* riddled with feudal, monar-
> chial, and clerical anachronisms....Paine not only divined
> but also *defined* his readers' views, strengthening their
> beliefs, detonating their prejudices, touching their hearts,
> changing their minds, convincing them that they must
> speak out and act.[28]

It was a later book, *The Age of Reason*, however, in which
Paine in 1797 expressed his religious views, that aroused the ire
of the religious establishment. We shall return to this book later.

Franklin also became very friendly with Joseph Priestley,
an English scientist who later discovered the element oxygen.
Priestley was born in Yorkshire in 1733. His father was a textile
worker and a Dissenter, which was the term applied to those
Calvinists who dissented from the Church of England. As a youth,
Priestley read widely and by age 18 had rejected Calvinism in
favor of Arminianism (which did not subscribe to the Calvinist
doctrine of predestination.) Joseph was an avid student and
mastered not only Latin, Greek, and French but also High Dutch,
Italian, Hebrew, and some Syraic and Chaldee. He tried serving
as a minister at a dissenting church but changed to teaching at a
dissenting academy because a speech impediment, a slight
stammer, interfered with his preaching.[29] In 1766 he met
Franklin, who encouraged him to write a book on the history of
electricity, published the following year. Priestley was then living
near a brewery and began experimenting with carbon dioxide, a
waste gas. He dissolved the gas in water, liked the taste, and thus
invented soda water.[30] Priestley continued his scientific experi-

ments continued over the next decade. In 1774, in what he described as a chance discovery, he produced the element oxygen (which he termed "dephlogistcated air) from mercuric oxide.

During subsequent years, Priestley's religious thinking became more and more critical of established church doctrines. Like David Hume, he rejected free will, miracles, and the Trinity. He did, however, continue to believe in God, based on the theory of divine design, and was ambivalent about life after death.[31] His biographer Anne Holt states, "Priestly's theological opinions show steady development; from Calvinism he passed to Arminianism, from Arminianism to Arianism, and finally Socinianism."[32] As the reader will recall from the previous chapter, the Socinians, like the Unitarians, rejected the divinity of Jesus.

Franklin spent his last day in London before his return to America in March 1775 alone with Priestley from morning until night.[33] Priestley himself, however, did not come to America until 1794, after his neighbors had burned down his house because of his heretical views. After his arrival in America, he was targeted by Alexander Hamilton as an undesirable alien and threatened with deportation under the Alien and Sedition Acts. Fortunately, President John Adams, who had a generally favorable opinion of Priestly, called off any action. Adams wrote to his wife, Abigail, in March 1796, "I am going to hear Dr. Priestley. His discourses are learned, ingenious, and useful."[34] Eventually the accession of Jefferson to the presidency removed the threat of deportation.[35] Priestley established Unitarian congregations in both Philadelphia and in Northumberland, Pennsylvania, where he had settled, but neither society endured. He died in February 1804.

Strictly speaking, Priestley was not a deist, for he continued to hold many Christian beliefs, such as the resurrection of Jesus and other miracles.[36] In fact he strongly disapproved of Paine's deistic beliefs and wrote several tracts denouncing them. Nevertheless, we have included him in this book because he was the founder of the Unitarian church in America, because of his friendship with Jefferson, who was both a deist and a Unitarian, and because in the nineteenth century many Unitarians were deists or atheists.

Franklin's own religious views toward the end of his life are expressed in a letter he wrote in 1790 (the year of his death) to Ezra Stiles, the president of Yale College, who had queried Franklin on his religious beliefs:

> As to Jesus of Nazareth, my opinion of whom you particularly desire, I think the system of morals and his religion, as he left them to us, the best the world ever saw or is likely to see, but I apprehend it has received various corrupting changes, and I have, with most of the present dissenters in England, some doubts as to his divinity....I have ever let others enjoy their religious sentiments, without reflecting on them for those that appeared to me to be insupportable, and even absurd.[37]

Franklin's expressed doubts about the divinity of Jesus and his rejection of the Calvinistic doctrine of determinism have convinced some writers that Franklin was basically a deist. Herbert Morais writes in *Deism in Eighteenth Century America*:

> In spite of his reticence in respect to deism, Franklin said enough, chiefly in confidential letters, to warrant his classification as a deist....Franklin was persuaded that reason was to be used to ascertain the basic principles of a sound religion. These fundamental truths consisted of a belief in the existence of God, of the practice of virtue, and the immortality of the soul....Felicity was to be achieved through the good life, which was more important to the success of religion than was orthodoxy....Although he did not desire to see Christian influence diminished, Franklin thought that his creed did nor require the support of supernatural evidences.[38]

We shall now turn to the third member of the Committee formed to write the Declaration of Independence, John Adams. Adams was born in 1735 in Braintree, Massachusetts, a suburb of Boston, and entered Harvard College in 1751, intending to go into the ministry. As he notes in his autobiography, however, he perceived "that the study of theology and the pursuit of it as a profession would involve me in endless altercations and make my life miserable, without any prospect of doing good to my fellow men,"[39] so he decided to become a lawyer. This decision was prompted in part by Adams' observation of the treatment in Braintree of the Reverend Lemuel Briant, the Congregational minister. Briant's unorthodox religious views split the town and the Adams family. Much to the dismay of his father, John sided with Briant.[40]

Briant embraced the anti-Calvinist doctrine of Arminianism, which rejected Calvin's teaching of predestination and maintained salvation was possible for all. Briant held that "man was a responsible agent whose happiness depended on his personal actions. To disparage moral goodness was to promote infidelity, to encourage vice, and to remove divine comfort. The very aim of God was to advance happiness in man."[41] In many ways, the position of the Arminians was similar to that of the deists in that both believed in the power of reason to establish religious beliefs. The Arminians, however, while believing in natural religion, also accepted the revealed religion of Christianity.[42]

Adams, while not wanting to become a minister, did not have the money required to spend several years in a lawyer's office preparing for the bar. Accordingly, he took a position as a Latin teacher in a grammar school in Worcester, and the town paid for his room and board. In the boarding house he later related that he "found Morgan's *Moral Philosopher*, which I was informed had circulated with some freedom in that town, and that the principles of deism had made considerable progress among several persons in that and other towns in the county."[43]

Morgan was an English deist who wrote *The Moral Philosopher* in 1737, in which he asserted that "Christianity, as first practiced by Jesus, was in reality deism. He held that the simple teachings of Christ had been corrupted by his followers, who had altered the gospels and ascribed miracles to his doctrines."[44]

Three months after he arrived in Worcester, Adams met socially a local lawyer named James Putnam, a brilliant attorney with somewhat unorthodox views. During his first meeting with Putnam, at a gathering of other men, Adams heard the attorney declare to a minister:

> It is my opinion that the apostles were nothing more than a company of enthusiasts. We are told that they spoke with different tongues, healed the sick, and raised the dead. But we have only their word. What kind of evidence is that, after seventeen hundred years? A court of law would throw out their case, *nulli prosequi.*[45]

Adams continued to meet with Putnam and in, August 1756, accepted an offer to study law in Putnam's office after teaching at his school and to board at Putnam's house. He spent a very busy two years instructing his students in the morning and being instructed in the law in the afternoon. Adams also took advantage of Putnam's library, which included works by Bolingbroke.[46] In 1758 he returned to Boston, where he was sworn in as an attorney at law.

For the next decade Adams acted as a lawyer in Boston and surrounding towns, marrying Abigail Smith in August 1764. In 1774, after serving in the Massachusetts House of Representatives, Adams was appointed one of the five delegates from Massachusetts to the First Continental Congress. At the second Congress, he met Franklin and Jefferson and was appointed with them to the committee that wrote the Declaration of Independence.

Following the Second Continental Congress, all three men eventually were sent to Europe as representatives of the colonies. Franklin was the first to go, leaving for France with Silas Deane and Arthur Lee in October 1776. The following January the three commissioners formally requested French aid, which was granted. As mentioned above, Franklin was a member of the Masonic Order and quickly associated with the Masonic Lodge of the Nine Sisters in Paris. There he assisted with the initiation of Voltaire in March 1778 and officiated at Voltaire's Masonic funeral service in November of the same year.[47]

In April 1778, Adams replaced Silas Deane as a minister to France. Initially, Adams occupied part of Franklin's house, and his son, John Quincy Adams, then ten, went to school with Franklin's grandson, Benjamin Bache. This stay in France was followed by a series of other diplomatic assignments before he finally returned home in 1788. Neither Adams nor his wife, Abigail, who joined him in London, appear to have been influenced by the religious views of the men they met abroad.

Adams served as Vice President under President George Washington during both of Washing-ton's terms and was elected President in his own right in 1800, with Jefferson as his Vice President. (The Constitution originally provided that the candidate receiving the most votes in the Electoral College should become President, with the runner-up assuming the office of Vice President. The Constitution did not foresee political parties, so the administration of Federalist John Adams had a Vice President, Jefferson, from the opposition Republican party.[a])

During Adams' term as President, a treaty was signed with the Barbary Pirates of Tripoli to end their attacks on

-----

[a] Under Andrew Jackson, the Republicans became Democratic Republicans to distinguish themselves from John Quincy Adams' National Republicans and later shortened the Democratic Republicans to Democrats.

American ships. The treaty, passed by the U.S. Senate and signed by President Adams on June 10, 1797, stated in Article XI:

> As the government of the United States is not in any sense founded on the Christian religion—as it has in itself no character of enmity against the laws, religion or tranquility of the Mussulmen—and as the said states never have entered into any war or act of hostility against any Mahometan nation, it is declared by the parties that no pretext arising from religious opinions shall ever produce an interruption of the harmony existing between the two countries.[48]

This document is often quoted by religious liberals to counter claims by the contemporary Christian Right that the United States was founded as a Christian nation

Now to return to Jefferson. After the proclamation of the Declaration, Jefferson returned to Virginia. He resigned from the Continental Congress, but continued to work in the Virginia legislature for a series of reforms, which included a bill for the disestablishment of the Church of England and complete religious freedom. A portion of this bill that exempted dissenters from the religious tax was passed, but the balance of Jefferson's proposals on religious freedom had to wait until 1786 for passage.[49]

On June 1, 1779, Jefferson was elected wartime governor of Virginia to succeed Patrick Henry. He continued as governor for two one-year terms during the most difficult days of the Revolution. At one point, Governor Jefferson had to flee Monticello to escape capture by the British, who subsequently sacked the house, looting the library and drinking his best wine.[50] During the period that he was governor, Jefferson wrote his only book, *Notes on the State of Virginia,* written as a reply to a query from a member of the French legation in America about the customs and the cultures of the various states. The book contained one section on religion which was used against Jefferson by his

43

political opponents, the Federalists, during the 1800 presidential campaign as conclusive evidence that Jefferson was some combination of pagan, infidel, atheist, and heretic. In the book, Jefferson wrote:

> The legitimate powers of government extend to such acts only as are injurious to others. But it does me no injury for my neighbor to say there are twenty Gods or no God. It neither picks my pocket nor breaks my leg...Difference of opinion is advantageous in religion. The several sects perform the office of *censor morum* over each other.[51]

Jefferson did not run for a third term as governor but was elected to Congress in 1783. He became an active force, writing some thirty-one major reports and drafting the ordinance for the governance of the new Northwest Territories. On the other hand, he lost the vote to exclude slavery from the new territory by one vote. He was ready to leave Congress by May 1784, when he was appointed a minister to France to replace John Jay. Because Jefferson's wife, Martha, had died the previous year, he took his daughter Martha (known as Patsy) to Paris with him.

Jefferson's religious views at that period in his life are explained in a letter to his nephew Peter Carr, written in 1787 while he was in Paris:

> Those facts in the Bible which contradict the laws of nature must be examined with care, and under a variety of faces...Do not be frightened from this enquiry by any fear of its consequences. If it ends in a belief that there is no god, you will find incitements to virtue in the comfort and pleasantness you feel in its exercise, and the love of others which it will procure you. If you find reason to believe there is a god, a consciousness that you are acting under his eye, and that he approves you, will be a vast additional incitement....Your own reason is the only oracle

given you by heaven, and you are answerable not for the rightness but uprightness of the decision.

When Jefferson and Patsy arrived in Paris, they were helped by John and Abigail Adams, just as Adams and his son, John Quincy, on their arrival had been helped by Franklin. Abigail was especially important in helping Jefferson during a long illness in his first winter in Paris. She also persuaded Jefferson to bring his younger daughter, Mary (known as Polly), who was only four, to France.[52] Adams and Jefferson together negotiated a loan of $400,000 from the Dutch to the new republic, but otherwise Jefferson accomplished little of substance during his French stay. He did, however, thoroughly enjoy French food, French wine, and French architecture. Patsy, whom Jefferson had placed in a convent school, was even more enamored of France and announced to her father that she had decided to become a nun and remain in France. Horrified, Jefferson removed her from the convent the following day. Not long afterward, Jefferson returned to America with his daughters, expecting to come back to France after a few months in Monticello. Once home, however, he accepted President Washington's invitation to become the nation's first Secretary of State.

While Jefferson was in Paris, he relied on his fellow Virginian James Madison to keep him apprised of the events at the Constitutional Convention in Philadelphia. Jefferson and Madison had first worked together in the Virginia Convention of 1776, which was called to draft a new constitution for the state. Madison had proposed an amendment, supported by Jefferson, declaring that all men were entitled to the free exercise of religion. Although the amendment was defeated, the two men did succeed in exempting dissenters from having to pay taxes to the established church.[53] Ten years later, in 1786, Madison was instrumental in obtaining passage by the Virginia Assembly of the Bill for Religious Freedom, which Jefferson had drafted before he went to France. The document contained this paragraph:

ATHEISTS, AGNOSTICS, AND DEISTS IN AMERICA

No man shall be compelled to frequent or support any religious worship, place, or ministry whatsoever... nor shall be enforced, restrained, molested, or burdened in his body or goods, or shall otherwise suffer on account of his religious opinions or belief; but that all men shall be free to profess, and by argument to maintain, their opinions in matters of religion, and that the same shall in no wise diminish, enlarge, or affect their civil capacities.[54]

Madison represented Virginia at the Constitutional Convention in Philadelphia in 1788-1789, at which religion was not a major subject for debate. Article VI of the Constitution, however, which required all federal and state officials to take an oath supporting the Constitution, included the phrase, "no religious test shall ever be required as a qualification to any office or public trust under the United States."[55] After the adoption of the Constitution, Madison took the lead in having the Bill of Rights introduced in the first Congress, with the First Amendment guaranteeing the separation of church and state. The Bill of Rights received the necessary two-thirds vote in the House and Senate and was ratified by the states in 1791. In the first Congress, Madison also tried to prevent the congressional chaplains from being paid out of the public treasury, but his attempt failed.[56]

Jefferson returned from Paris hoping to retire to Monticello. Instead, he became involved in the new government of the United States. After serving as Secretary of State under Washington from 1790 to 1793, he was elected Vice President under John Adams in 1796 and was elected President of the United States in 1800. Jefferson served as President for eight years, during which time he was responsible for the Louisiana Purchase. As his Secretary of State, Jefferson chose Madison, who in turn assumed the presidency in 1809.

Only two weeks after his inauguration as President,

ATHEISM AND DEISM IN THE NEW REPUBLIC

Jefferson created a political stir by offering passage on a government ship to Tom Paine, who had barely escaped the guillotine in France for backing the wrong faction in the French Revolution and who was trying to return to America. The opposition to using government money to this end was not caused by Paine's reputation as a patriot during the Revolution but by his book *The Age of Reason*, written in France and published in America. Paine had written the book to reawaken the faith of the French in God, since so many Frenchmen had become atheists. In the book, however, he advocated a return to simplicity of worship, "unshackled by the fables of books pretending to be the word of God." Since he included the Bible as one of the "fables", *The Age of Reason* was widely interpreted as an attack on Christianity.[57] "Federalist newspaper editors had a field day describing 'the two Toms' walking arm in arm, allegedly comparing notes on the ideal way to promote atheism or their past successes in despoiling Christian virgins."[58]

Paine's *Age of Reason* became very popular with the students at both Harvard and Yale. The Reverend Lyman Beecher recalled that at Yale "most of the students were skeptical" and the college church was almost extinct. In Boston, Judge Daniel White wrote of "the infidel and irreligious spirit which prevailed at that period among the students at Cambridge." In 1796 Harvard presented each student with a copy of Watson's *Apology for the Bible* as an antidote to *The Age of Reason*. Many ministers preached sermons claiming that Paine was part of a conspiracy to supplant Christianity with the Cult of Reason.[59]

In spite of the virulent public criticism, Jefferson and Paine remained loyal friends. Paine, however, attacked the former President, John Adams, emphasizing the shallowness of Adams' judgment and accusing him of "consummate vanity."[60] The dislike was mutual. Adams wrote of Paine in an 1810 letter to the Philadelphia physician Benjamin Rush:

His political writings, I am singular enough to believe,

have done more harm than his irreligious ones. He understood neither government nor religion....His deism, it appears to me, has promoted rather than retarded the cause of revolution in America....The Christian religion, as I understand it, is the brightness of the glory and express portrait of the character of the eternal..., self-existent, independent, benevolent, all-powerful and all merciful creator....It will last as long as the world.[61]

In 1804, while still in the White House, Jefferson began a project of editing the New Testament to recover "the pure and unsophisticated doctrines of Jesus." He did this by means of a cut-and-paste process of editing the four Gospels that highlighted the parables and ethical teaching of Jesus, while excising or minimizing miracles and theology. The result was the "Jefferson Bible," which he titled *The Life and Morals of Jesus*. He felt that this book showed that he himself was "a real Christian, that is to say a disciple of the doctrines of Jesus."[62]

In spite of their disagreements on Tom Paine, Jefferson and Adams shared many of the same religious views. Both men believed that organized religion with its sectarian dogmas was an obstacle to the search for religious truth. In one of his letters to a friend, Adams wrote:

The Priesthood have in all ancient nations, nearly monopolized learning.... And, even since the Reformation, when or where has existed a Protestant or dissenting sect who would tolerate A FREE INQUIRY? The blackest billingsgate, the most ungentlemanly insouciance, the most yahooish brutality is patiently endured, countenanced, propagated and applauded. But touch a solemn truth in collision with the dogma of a sect, though capable of the clearest truth, and you will soon find you have disturbed a nest, and the hornets will swarm about legs and hands and fly into your face and eyes. [63]

In a similar vein, Jefferson wrote to Adams in 1813:

> It is too late in the day for men of sincerity to pretend they believe in Platonic mysticisms....But this constitutes the craft, the power and the profit of the priests. Sweep away the gossamer fabrics of factitious religion and they would catch no more flies. We should all then, like the Quakers, live without an order of priests, moralize for ourselves, follow the oracle of conscience, and say nothing about what no man can understand, nor therefore believe, for I suppose belief to be the assent of the mind to an intelligible proposition.[64]

Further, both men believed in the unity of God and rejected the doctrine of the Trinity. Adams continued to refer to "the God of nature," as in the following 1815 letter to Jefferson:

> The question before the human race is whether the God of nature shall govern the world by His own laws, or whether priests and kings shall rule it by fictitious miracles? Or, in other words, whether authority is originally in the people? Or whether it has descended for 1800 years in a succession of popes and bishops, or brought down from heaven by the Holy Ghost in the form of a dove in a phial of holy oil?[65]

James Madison also used the phrase "Nature's God" in his letter to Frederick Beasley in 1825. Beasley had sent Madison a copy of a religious tract he had authored which used several of the standard arguments to prove the existence of God. Madison replied:

> But whatever effect may be produced on some minds by the more abstract ideas which you so strongly support, it will probably always be found that the course of reasoning from the effect to the cause, "from Nature to Nature's God"

will be the more universal and persuasive application.[66]

Madison's biographer Irving Brant characterizes Madison's religious beliefs as "a quiet unorthodoxy differing more in manner than in matter from the housetop-shouting deism of Jefferson."[67] In 1815, while he was President, Madison had as a dinner guest a young man from Boston, George Tichnor, who was touring America in preparation for a trip to Europe. Tichnor wrote his father:

> He talked of religious sects and parties and was curious to know how the cause of liberal Christianity stood with us and if the Athanasian creed was well received by us Episcopalians. He pretty distinctly intimated to me his own regard for the Unitarian doctrine.[68]

Jefferson was not formally affiliated with the Unitarian church, but he attended Priestley's Unitarian church when he was in Philadelphia and corresponded frequently with Unitarian friends. Jefferson also believed in a rosy future for Unitarianism. His biographer Edwin Gaustad quotes him:

> "No one sees with greater pleasure than myself," he wrote in 1822, "the progress of reason in its advance towards rational Christianity." And the next year, he affirmed his "trust that there is not a young man living in the U.S. who will not die a Unitarian." To a former Methodist, now turned Unitarian, he added later that same year, "I confidently expect that the present generation will see Unitarianism become the general religion of the United States."[69]

Jefferson, of course, was completely mistaken in his forecast of the future of Unitarianism, although its doctrine and the deistic philosophy of some of its adherents did make progress in America in the nineteenth century. This we shall examine in a later chapter

In what Adams' son, John Quincy Adams, termed "a strange and striking coincidence," both Adams and Jefferson died on July 4, 1826, the fiftieth anniversary of the signing of the Declaration of Independence.[70] Jefferson was buried at his beloved Monticello. Adams lies with his wife Abigail and his son John Quincy in a crypt in the basement of the First Parish Church (Unitarian) in Quincy, Massachusetts.[71]

Of course, the founding fathers were not the only Americans with deistic tendencies in the late eighteenth century. Ethan Allen, the leader of the Green Mountain boys and the hero of the battle at Fort Ticonderoga during the Revolution, was an avowed deist, introduced to deism by an English physician, Thomas Young. Allen later wrote an anti-Christian book titled *Reason, Pthe Only Oracle of Man."* In the introduction to the book, he states, "I have generally been denominated a Deist, the reality of which I have never disputed."[72] The book rejected not only the doctrine of the Trinity but also the Biblical accounts of the creation, the validity of prophesies, and the possibility of miracles. Allen's book embraced "natural religion" based on reason. Although a fire in the printer's storeroom destroyed most of the copies of the book, the copies that remained circulated widely.[73]

Deism in the closing years of the eighteenth century was not confined to the national political leadership. In Windham County, Connecticut, the county historian reports that in 1795 the majority of the people were deists.[74] When the General Assembly of the Presbyterian Church met in Philadelphia in 1798, it predicted that unless Americans turned away from deism, the wrath of God would be visited upon them.[75]

Prominent among the nonpolitical deists was Elihu Palmer, who was born in Connecticut in 1764. After graduating from Dartmouth in 1787 with a Phi Beta Kappa key, he decided to enter the ministry.[76] Apparently during his college years, he became exposed to Epicurean philosophy, with its emphasis on happiness as the goal of human life. On the way to his first ministerial post in the village of Newtown on Long Island, he preached a Thanksgiving service at Sheffield, Massachusetts. A friend, John Fellows, recalled late that

> Instead of expatiating upon the horrid and awful condition of mankind in consequence of the lapse of Adam and his wife, he exhorted his hearers to spend the day joyfully in innocent festivity, and to render themselves as happy as possible.[77]

Because of his heretical views, Palmer lasted only six months in Newtown and scarcely longer at his next post in Philadelphia. He then became the minister in that same city of the Universal Society, founded by John Fitch, one of the inventors of the steamboat. After Palmer delivered a sermon denying the divinity of Christ, though, the Episcopal bishop of Philadelphia used his influence to prevent the owner of the building used by the Universal Society for its services from allowing Palmer and his congregation to use it in the future.[78] Threatened with violence, Palmer left the city to stay with his brother in western Pennsylvania. There he studied law and returned to Philadelphia in 1793, where he was admitted to the bar. Unfortunately, three months later he lost both his wife and his sight in a yellow fever epidemic, ending his legal career.[79]

Now blind, Palmer resumed the preaching of deism, first in Augusta, Georgia, and then in New York City in 1794. In the latter city, he spoke before a radical offshoot of the Tammany Society. Some of his listeners were so impressed that they decided to aid the blind clergyman and founded the Deistical Society for that purpose in the winter of 1796-97. The constitution of the organization, drawn up by Palmer, urged its members to oppose "all schemes of superstition and fanaticism claiming divine origin."[80] The society had financial difficulties, since it principally relied for its revenue on dues of six cents per meeting, and the organization died in the early 1800s.

Palmer also preached to the Druidical Society of Newburgh, New York, a town fifty miles north of New York City. This offshoot of a local Masonic lodge adopted its name under the assumption that "they were returning to the pure worship of the sun from which both Christianity and Freemasonry were derived." In addition to offering lectures by Palmer, the society distributed copies of Paine's *Age of Reason*.[81] Palmer also helped organize a deistic society in Baltimore. The membership of these societies was drawn largely from the lower social classes, particularly printers and booksellers. These societies, like Palmer's earlier efforts, were short-lived. The religious historian Adolph Koch comments, "Palmer's rationalistic Deism was unable to compete with the emotional lure of evangelical revivalism."[82]

In spite of his blindness, Palmer also wrote books, the best known of which is *Principles of Nature: A Development of the Moral Causes of Happiness and Misery among the Human Species,* published in 1801. In this work, Palmer acknowledged his debt to the writings of Voltaire, Hume, and Bolingbroke, deists discussed in the previous chapter of this history. Palmer rejected the prophesies and miracles reported in the Bible, as well as the divinity of Jesus. His attack on the Bible and organized religion in *Principles of Nature* was strong and encompassed Judaism, Christianity, and Islam. He wrote:

> Moses and Mahomet governed their followers with a rod of iron, and a military despotism. They were savage and ferocious men, crafty and intriguing, and they knew how to subject to their will the stupid but unfortunate followers who were devoted to their views. If Jesus was more mild, benevolent, and temperate, it was because he had less power, and because his disposition was less cruel and resentful. His followers, when clothed with power, have not paid a very high compliment to their master, for the

history of their conduct evinces the most malignant design, and the earth has been drenched in blood to defend their religion, of which the meek and lowly Jesus is reputed to be the author.[83]

Palmer's critical view of the Bible also led him to reject the virgin birth of Jesus. Since Joseph believed his wife was a virgin and Palmer found the story of impregnation by the Holy Ghost unbelievable, he was led to conclude that for Christians, "their pretended Savior is nothing more than an illegitimate Jew, and their hopes of salvation through him rest on no better foundation than that of fornication or adultery."[84]

It is no wonder that Palmer's radical views failed to gain financial support from the wealthy in the communities in which he organized deistic societies. None of them survived his 1806 death in Philadelphia from pleurisy while on a speaking tour. His writings survived, however, in the libraries of many influential Americans, including that of Thomas Jefferson. [85]

It should be noted that Palmer was a deist rather than an atheist—he believed that the universe was originally set in motion by a Creator. In fact, none of the men we have discussed in this chapter were atheists, although many were accused of being so. Tom Paine, in particular, was called an atheist not only in his lifetime but a century later. Theodore Roosevelt in 1888 wrote of Paine as a "filthy little atheist" and said that he was the kind of infidel who "esteems a bladder of dirty water as the proper weapon to assail Christianity."[86]

During the 1800 presidential campaign, Jefferson was branded an atheist by his Federalist opponents. Even George Washington was suspected of being at least a deist, if not an atheist, because he did not take communion, and when his wife Martha did, he waited for her outside the church.[87]

If the reader is disappointed that we have not yet encountered an American atheist, be assured that they will emerge in the next chapter.

CHAPTER IV

FANNY WRIGHT, ROBERT OWEN, AND THE COMMUNITARIANS

We opened the previous chapter with a review of the life and religious views of Thomas Jefferson, one of the best-known Americans. In contrast, this chapter will start with the life and religious views of Frances (Fanny) Wright, a name that few Americans will now recognize. We shall refer to her as "Fanny" to distinguish her from her sister Camilla and from Elizur Wright, an abolitionist and atheist, who also will be discussed in this book. (There was no relation between the two.)

One hundred and fifty years ago Fanny was famous both in the United States and abroad. Jefferson filled seven pages of his commonplace book with passages from one of her works[1] and invited her to spend some time in Monticello, which she did in the company of the Marquis de Lafayette.[2] She also was received cordially by Andrew Jackson at his estate, the Hermitage.[3] Walt Whitman wrote of her, "We all loved her; fell down before her; her very appearance seemed to enthrall us."[4] In Europe she had warm friendships with Jeremy Bentham in England and Lafayette in France

Fanny was born in Dundee, Scotland, in 1795, but was brought up in London by her maternal grandfather and aunt Frances after both her parents died when she was only two and a half years old. At the age of eight, she and her sister, Camilla, who had remained with relatives in Dundee, inherited a sizable fortune from an uncle who died in India. The money allowed the two sisters and their aunt Frances to move to the Devonshire coast. As soon as Fanny reached age eighteen, the two sisters moved again, this time back to Scotland, where they lived with their uncle James Mylne in Glasgow. Mylne was both a minister in the Church of Scotland and a professor of moral philosophy at Glasgow University, occupying the chair formerly held by Adam Smith. Mylne was known by his students as "Old Sensation" because he took the position of John Locke that our knowledge is based on evidence provided by our senses. Fanny adopted her uncle's position.[5]

She had free access to her uncle's extensive library as well as to that of the university. She and some friends formed a group that met at intervals to discuss literature and philosophy, as well as to read each other their compositions. For this group Fanny wrote an essay on Epicurean philosophy, later published as *A Few Days in Athens*. It is in the form of conversations between Epicurus and two students, Theon and Leontium, Epicurus' first female disciple. Leontium (modeled after Fanny herself) learns to honor happiness as a virtue, a garden as a place of beauty, and refined pleasure as the goal of life. "To be happy, we must be virtuous; and when we are virtuous, we are wise."[6] This Epicurean philosophy served as a basis for the deism which she espoused throughout her life.

Fanny also read extensively about America; was fascinated by what she read; and decided in 1818 to sail to the United States with Camilla. Through letters of introduction from their Scottish relatives, the sisters met many important New Yorkers, including Charles Wilkes, the future president of the Bank of New York, and David Colden, the son of Mayor Cadwallader Colden. Fanny even managed to have a play titled *Altdorf*, which she had written back in Scotland, produced on Broadway to favorable reviews. The play was also later staged in Philadelphia, again to favorable reviews. The Wrights' American stay included travels to Niagara Falls and Washington, D.C. There they met Henry Clay, Speaker of the House, and were introduced to President James Monroe.[7] The sisters also filed for U.S. citizenship but, nevertheless, decided to return to Europe and sailed from New York in May 1820 for England.[8] They did not return until 1824.

During her tour of the United States, Fanny took copious notes, which she later published as *Views of Society and Manners in America*. The book contained one chapter on religion, which included the following paragraph:

> You will conceive how great is the change wrought in the religious temper of the eastern states, when I mention that the Unitarian faith has lately been introduced and, in some parts, has made such rapid progress as promises, ere long, to supersede the doctrines of Calvin. There were, of course, some vehement pulpit fulminations in Massachusetts when these mild teachers of morals and simple Christianity first made their appearance. But fortunately, Calvin could no longer burn Servetus,[a] however much he might scold at him...[9]

In the concluding chapter of the book, Fanny expresses her views on slavery, which she acted on during her next trip. She wrote, "The sight of slavery is revolting everywhere, but to inhale the impure breath of its pestilence in the free winds of America is odious beyond all that the imagination can conceive."

Fanny spent most of the four years in France as the guest of the Marquis de Lafayette, whose wife had recently died. The pair was rumored to be lovers, although her biographer, Celia Eckhardt, concludes that it was a paternal relationship. At any rate, they were very close. Lafayette had her portrait painted and hung it in his study. He wrote her notes, such as "Tomorrow, at four o'clock at the latest, my beloved Fanny will again be in the arms of her paternal friend, who loves her as she deserves to be

---

[a] A Spanish theologian and physician with Unitarian views who was burned at the stake in Geneva in 1553.

loved."[10]

When Lafayette traveled to America in 1775 to help with the celebration of the fiftieth anniversary of the Declaration of Independence, Fanny and Camilla also visited, though for propriety's sake they sailed on a separate boat. The two sisters accompanied Lafayette on part of his triumphal tour. In Washington, they met Robert Owen, an Englishman who was to loom as large in Fanny's future life as the Frenchman Lafayette had in her past. Owen had gone to work at age seven and through hard work and an entrepreneurial spirit by age twenty-eight had become part owner and manager of the cotton mill and surrounding village of New Lanark near the Falls of Clyde south of Glasgow in Scotland. He decided to use the mill and community around it to demonstrate that it was economically feasible to have an industrial society without exploitation of the workers. In the cotton mill which Owen managed, he stopped the use of child labor, shortened working hours, and provided the workers with clean, affordable housing. The mill's profitability increased and "Owenism" was born. He failed, however, to persuade his fellow manufacturers to adopt his reforms and decided that America might be more receptive to his ideas.[11]

Owen's religious views are stated in detail in his autobiography. He wrote:

All the religions of the world are based on total ignorance of all the fundamental laws of humanity, and of the facts of undeviating perpetual occurrence....Fully conscious as I am of the misery which these religions have created in the human race, which they now create, and which they must create while supported by the authorities of the world..., I would now, if I possessed ten thousand lives and could suffer a painful death for each, willingly thus sacrifice them to destroy this Moloch"[12]

FANNY WRIGHT AND ROBERT OWEN

Owen was not, however, an atheist but rather a deist. He believed in religious toleration and urged the villagers in New Lanark "to the utmost of their power as far as is consistent with their duty to God and society, to endeavor both by word and deed to make everyone happy with whom they have any intercourse."[13]

When Fanny met Owen in Washington, he had just completed the purchase of a community in Indiana called Harmonie from a group of German immigrants under the leadership of a charismatic figure named George Rapp. The group styled itself as primitive Christians and had decided to sell the village and move to Pennsylvania. Owen paid $125,000 for the Rappite establishment, which comprised 20,000 acres of land, of which 2,000 were under cultivation. The buildings included houses, two churches, four mills, a textile factory, a distillery, a brewery, a tannery, and mechanics' shops.[14] On this site, he proposed to establish what became known as an "Owenite" community, although he did not use the name. Owen issued a general invitation to "the industrious and well-disposed of all nations" to come to the place he had renamed New Harmony, and about 800 people showed up.[15] A constitution was adopted in May 1825, which established a governing committee named by Owen. The organization was socialist in nature, with the inhabitants contributing their labor and receiving in return an annual credit at the community store of $180.[16]

Owen invited Fanny to visit New Harmony, the former Rappite community. Fanny accepted the invitation, and she and Camilla journeyed by stagecoach across the Alleghenies, down the Ohio by steamboat, and by horseback from the small Ohio River port of Mount Vernon, Indiana, to New Harmony. Fanny was much impressed by what had been accomplished by the Germans under George Rapp before Owen's purchase. During her travels, Fanny had been dismayed at the institution of slavery and sought a remedy. In subsequent months after her visit to New Harmony, she conceived the idea of a colony which could demonstrate that slaves could live in a similar community and earn the money to purchase their freedom. She consulted Lafayette and Governor De Witt Clinton of New York, both of whom endorsed her plan.[17] She now had to decide where to establish the proposed venture. She found that Tennessee was the most liberal of the slave states, with twenty antislavery societies. Lafayette wrote a letter of introduction to Andrew Jackson on her behalf.[18]

In the fall of 1825, Fanny traveled to Tennessee and was cordially received by Jackson at his estate, the Hermitage. With his help, she purchased 320 acres of land on the Wolf River for $480 and chose the Chickasaw Indian name for the river, Nashoba, as the name for her future colony. She also recruited two men to help her in the new enterprise—George Flowers, an Englishman whom she had met in New Harmony, and James Richardson, a Scotsman she met in Memphis. Finally, she purchased ten slaves, six men and four women.[19]

Camilla soon joined them, and initially Nashoba seemed to go well. The slaves worked hard without the threat of whipping, and the small community appeared to visitors to be clean and orderly. Fanny had time to add several chapters to *A Few Days in Athens*. From the contents of these chapters, she appears in the intervening years to have changed from a deist to an atheist. She wrote:

> Surely the absurdity of all other doctrines of religion, and the iniquity of many, are sufficiently evident. To fear a being on account of his power is degrading; to fear him if he is good, ridiculous....I see no sufficient evidence of his existence; and to reason of its possibility, I hold to be an idle speculation.[20]

Fanny returned to New Harmony in May and June of 1826. Robert Owen was there as was William Maclure, a fellow deist who had invested in New Harmony. The historian Arthur Bestor writes that Owen "found himself in the midst of a group who avowed their deistic views with an openness and militancy he had not met with before." On July Fourth, Owen gave an oration entitled "A Declaration of Mental Independence" which advocated freeing mankind from the bonds of private property, the institution of marriage, and "absurd and irrational systems of religion."[21] Although the leadership of New Harmony held deistic beliefs, the majority of the residents did not. One of the two churches built by the Rappites was put to secular use, but the other was available without charge to any minister who asked for it, regardless of his religious views. One Sunday a member proposed ejecting a visiting preacher who attacked Owen as the anti-Christ, but Owen himself rose to defend the man's freedom of speech.[22]

Unfortunately, Fanny became ill after she got back to Nashoba. She decided to return to Europe for her health and arranged to travel with Robert Dale Owen, Robert Owen's son. While she was gone, Camilla and James Richardson were left in charge. Unfortunately, Richardson was not the leader that Fanny was and he soon resorted to whippings to control the slaves. Further, he took one of the slaves as a mistress and mentioned this in an article on Nashoba published in a Baltimore journal, *The Genius of Universal Emancipation*. One of the newspaper's readers wrote a letter to the editor which denounced Nashoba as "one great brothel." Richardson replied, "I have seen a brothel, and I never knew a place so unlike it as Nashoba". He added, "I am an Atheist, and on the diffusion of Atheism rests my only hope of the progress of Universal Emancipation."[23]

Meanwhile in Europe, Fanny and Robert Dale Owen tried to recruit additional members for the Nashoba commune. Fanny visited Mary Shelley, widow of the poet Percy Bysshe Shelley. Since Mary was also the daughter of William Godwin, the author of *Political Justice* and a proponent of the overthrow of all oppressive institutions such as government, religion, and private property, Fanny thought Mary would be a likely candidate for Nashoba. Mary, however, felt bound to England by her son, Percy. Nevertheless, Fanny did succeed in convincing Frances Trollope, mother of the novelist Anthony Trollope, to come back with her. The party included not only Mrs. Trollope but also her son, Henry, two servants, and a French artist.[24] They eventually reached Nashoba, where Mrs. Trollope received a real shock. She wrote in the draft of her book *Domestic Manners of the Americans*:

> When we arrived at Nashoba, they were without milk, without beverage of any kind except rain water, the river Wolf being too distant to send to constantly. Wheat bread they used but sparingly, and to us the Indian corn bread was uneatable. They had no vegetables but rice and some potatoes we brought with us, and no meat but pork....I shared her bedroom; it had no ceiling, and the floor consisted of planks laid loosely upon piles....The rain had access through the wooden roof, and the chimney caught fire at least a dozen times in a day, but Frances Wright stood in the midst of all this desolation, with the air of a conqueror; she would say, perhaps, that she was so, since she had conquered over all human weakness.[25]

Mrs. Trollope, naturally, soon left Nashoba. She subsequently made an extended tour of the United States, concentrating on the "domestic manners" described in her book. She was much impressed with the amount of religious activity, including revivals and camp meetings. She commented, however, on the number of nonbelievers, writing that "atheism is awake and thriving."[26] She also noted a conversation in a Cincinnati family she visited. "The girls used to say, 'Papa is an atheist,' just as they would have said of the multiform persuasions of their acquaintances, 'Mr. This is a Baptist.' and 'Mrs. That is a Methodist.'"[27] The implication of both remarks is that atheism was common enough to be considered within the usual range of beliefs of Americans at that time. On the other hand, another visitor to the United States, Alexis de Toqueville, who was sent to America by the French government in 1831 to examine prisons and penitentiaries, reported:

> While I was in America, a witness who happened to be
> called at the Sessions of the County of Chester (state of
> New York) declared that he did not believe in the exis-
> tence of God or in the immortality of the soul. The judge
> refused to admit his evidence, on the ground that the
> witness had destroyed beforehand all the confidence of the
> court in what he was about to say. The newspapers related
> the fact without any further comment.[28]

Returning to Fanny, she stayed in Nashoba until June,
when she left the commune in charge of an overseer and went to
New Harmony. There, she and Robert Owen analyzed the
Nashoba venture and concluded that it could not continue as a
cooperative community. The Nashoba experiment was essentially
dead. Eventually, Fanny took the ten slaves to Haiti and gave
them their freedom.[29]

In New Harmony, Fanny joined Robert Dale Owen as co-
editor of the weekly newspaper, the *New Harmony Gazette*. She
was also selected to give the July 4, 1828, address at New
Harmony. Fanny was probably the first woman in America to be
the main speaker at a public event for a mixed male-female
audience. She spoke in favor of liberty and equality, saying,
"Equality means, not the mere equality of political rights...but
equality of instruction and equality in virtue. Liberty means not
the mere voting at elections, but the free and fearless exercise of
mental facilities." The lecture was enthusiastically received.

Fanny decided that public speaking, in combination with
articles in the *Gazette*, would be a better way to convince the
public to adopt her views on emancipation, women's rights, and
religion than her project at Nashoba. Accordingly, the following
month she gave her second public lecture at the courthouse in
Cincinnati, Ohio. Frances Trollope attended this lecture. She
reported:

I was most anxious to hear her, but was almost deterred from attempting it by the reports that reached me of the immense crowd that was expected. After many consultations and hearing that many other ladies intended going, my friend Mrs. P**** and myself decided upon making the attempt, accompanied by a party of gentlemen, and found the difficulty less than we anticipated, though the building was crowded in every part. We congratulated ourselves that we had the courage to be among the number, for all my expectations fell far short of the splendour, the brilliance, the overwhelming eloquence of this extraordinary orator. Her lecture was upon the nature of true knowledge, and it contained little that could be objected to by any sect or party; it was intended as an introduction to the strange and startling theories contained in her subsequent lectures....[30]

Fanny gave two more lectures on subsequent Sundays, and they were so popular that she repeated them by special request at Cincinnati's theater. As noted by Mrs. Trollope, the first lecture was general, the second was based on the theories of Jeremy Bentham and Robert Owen, while the third contained strong attacks on the institution of marriage and on Christian churches and institutions.[31] Her lectures were so successful that she spent the next year and a half on the lecture circuit from New Orleans to Boston. At the conclusion of each lecture, she called for the creation in each community of a Hall of Science with an auditorium that would hold up to five thousand people, as well as a school, museum, and library. [32]

Fanny finally realized her plan for a Hall of Science in New York City in 1829. She was able to purchase the Ebenezer Baptist Church on Broome Street for $7,000 and renamed it the Hall of Science. The auditorium seated about twelve-hundred people, and lectures and debates were held each Sunday, as well as at intervals during the week. Fanny and Robert Dale Owen set up a bookstore in front of the building with their own books, as well as Tom Paine's deistic *Age of Reason* and tracts of the British radical Richard Carlile, who pioneered in birth control. The Hall of Science became a meeting place for liberal New Yorkers and visitors to the city. [33] Among the visitors was Robert Owen, who reported a series of debates he had held in Cincinnati with a Universalist minister, during which he claimed that he had converted many in the audience to the deist position.[34]

On the other hand, Owen's New Harmony experiment had not prospered. In March 1826 the village began to split apart into various entities: a School Society, an Agricultural and Pastoral Society, and a Mechanic and Manufacturing Society. The following year Owen tried to reorganize the whole community, but after he left in June 1827 New Harmony developed the rest of the way from communitarianism to individualism.[35]

A number of other settlements were established on the communitarian principles of Owen. These included the Yellow Springs Community in Ohio, on the site of the future Antioch College, the Haverstraw Community in Rockland County north of New York City, the Valley Forge Community in Pennsylvania, and three others in New York and Ohio. All, like Nashoba and New Harmony, failed.[36] The reasons for failure varied in each community. The common thread, however, was that the communitarian form of organization did not develop strong, effective leadership. In those communities which had strong leaders, such as Robert Owen in New Harmony and Fanny Wright in Nashoba, the leaders were absent for extended periods. In contrast, the Rappites who preceded Owen in New Harmony had an effective leader in Father Rapp, who did not travel extensively. Further, the Rappites, like the Amish and the Shakers, had a religious bond between the residents that the secular communities lacked.

Although Fanny's Nashoba experiment had failed and she did not establish any additional Halls of Science, she continued to be an effective lecturer. In Philadelphia on June 2, 1829, she gave a new lecture called "Of Existing Evils and Their Remedies."

In this speech she proposed that all children be placed in state-supported boarding schools where they would all eat the same food, wear the same clothes, and be taught the same subjects in a perfectly egalitarian way. Her critics charged that this scheme would undermine the institution of the family. Although she did not back down from the proposal, her later lectures that year went back to her themes of abolition of slavery, improved women's rights, and the errors of organized religion.[37] She spoke in Boston, Wilmington, and Providence to enthusiastic crowds.

This was, however, the peak of her career. On the trip to Haiti to free her slaves, mentioned above, Fanny had been accompanied by a teacher from New Harmony, William Phiquepal d'Arusmont. They became lovers, and Fanny found to her distress that she was pregnant. She went to Europe in the fall of 1830, and the baby was born in France in December or in January of the following year. To legitimatize the birth, she married Phiquepal in July 1831, with Lafayette as one of the witnesses.[38] It was not a happy marriage and eventually ended in divorce. Although Fanny returned to America, she never regained her former position of influence. She died in Cincinnati in 1852.

Thus, neither Robert Owen nor Fanny Wright left behind an organized movement to perpetuate their beliefs in the perfectibility of American society. They were not the only ones, though, attempting to change America. Another group of men and women, known as New England Transcendentalists, were also active in the first half of the nineteenth century, and in the next chapter we shall turn to them.

CHAPTER V

EMERSON, THOREAU, AND OTHER NEW ENGLAND TRANSCENDENTALISTS

The movement known as New England transcendentalism originated in 1836 in an organization in Boston called the Transcendental Club, which was organized for philosophical and literary, as well as religious, discussions. Some readers may question the inclusion of transcendentalists in a book primarily concerned with deists and atheists. On the other hand, many of the leading transcendentalists, including Ralph Waldo Emerson and Theodore Parker, were former Unitarian clergymen. The historian Paul Boller states, "Transcendentalism, in short, was mainly an enterprise undertaken by bright young Unitarians to find meaning, pattern, and purpose in a Universe no longer managed by a genteel and amiable Unitarian God."[1] Emerson left the denomination, while Parker remained a rebel within it, but both men shed the Unitarian beliefs in the Bible as a special authority and in a God who performed miracles, leaving the deistic core of a Creator, plus a reverence for Nature and an idealistic humanism. We shall examine the lives and the beliefs of these two men, as well as of Henry David Thoreau and Margaret Fuller.

The leader and chief spokesman of the transcendentalists was Emerson. Born in Boston on May 25, 1803, Waldo (as he later called himself) was the son of the Reverend William Emerson, a Unitarian minister. His father died when Waldo was eight, and he entered Boston Public Latin School the following year. He was a brilliant student and at age fourteen entered Harvard College as the youngest member of his class.[2] At Harvard Waldo waited on table for his board and did not, because of his poverty, join any of the prestigious clubs such as Porcellian or Hasty Pudding. His college record was not distinguished, although he did receive second prize for an essay submitted for the Bowdoin Prize in his senior year on "Present State of Ethical Philosophy." He graduated in 1821 at age eighteen, ranking thirtieth in his class of fifty-nine.[3]

Although he and his family decided he was destined to follow in his father's footsteps as a minister, Emerson also knew that he had to work several years to earn the money for tuition to divinity school. He applied as an instructor at his former school, Boston Latin, but was turned down because of his mediocre college record. He was then offered a job as assistant to his elder brother William, who ran a girls' school on Federal Street in Boston. Although Emerson did not particularly enjoy teaching, he had time to read extensively, including works by Hume and Priestley.[4] By 1825 he had saved sufficient money to enter Harvard Divinity School. At that time, the Divinity School did not have formal courses or grant degrees, so attendance involved residence at or near the university and supervised reading under direction of the faculty.[5]

In October 1826, Emerson met with the Middlesex Association of Unitarian Ministers and received his license to preach. During the next few years, he preached at a number of different Unitarian churches while waiting for a permanent "call," which he received in January 1829 from Boston's Second Church. In September of that year he married Ellen Tucker, who at age seventeen was nine years his junior and referred to him familiarly as "grandpa."[6] Unfortunately, at the time of their marriage Ellen was already ill from tuberculosis, and she died two years later.

During these years, Emerson was also reconsidering his theological beliefs. He became interested in the doctrines of Plotinus, the founder of Neoplatonism, whose works he read in translation. The Neoplatonists conceive of the world as an emanation from an ultimate being and that matter has no independent reality.[7] Emerson also studied astronomy and concluded that the earth was "an insignificant dot in boundless space" and that there must be other worlds inhabited by creatures who would not understand Christianity.[8]

Starting while he was still in Harvard, Emerson kept a journal. From this, we know that he was reading the Stoic writers, including Epictetus and Marcus Aurelius. The opening page of his 1822 *Journal World Wide* has an epigraph from Marcus Aurelius in Greek, which translated reads, "I seek the truth, whereby no one was ever harmed."[9] Over the next twenty years, the journals contain frequent quotations from Epictetus and Marcus Aurelius. Some of these Emerson later used in his essays, such as the quotation from Marcus Aurelius' *Meditations*, "It is pleasant to die, if there be gods; and sad to live, if there be none," which he used in both the essay "Worship" and in "Immortality."[10]

The differing philosophical backgrounds of Jefferson and Emerson can be seen by comparing their libraries. Jefferson's library contained a number of volumes by Epicurean writers, principally Lucretius;[11] Emerson's library had none. On the other hand, Emerson's library included two different translations of Marcus Aurelius' *Meditations*, as well as volumes of Epictetus. If Jefferson was an Epicurean, Emerson was a Stoic.

One result of Emerson's reading of the Stoic writers was his conclusion that Nature rather than the Bible was the best source of truth. In particular, he decided that Jesus had not intended the Last Supper to become a regular ritual of the church. His biographer Warren Staebler describes Emerson's thinking as follows:

> Communion needed to be seen as altogether a spiritual event; if things physical had no place in it, no more did symbols of things physical. Since it was altogether a spiritual event, no mediator had any place in it; it was not necessary that a Christian go through Jesus in order to get to God.[12]

ATHEISTS, AGNOSTICS, AND DEISTS IN AMERICA

In 1832, Emerson proposed to his church that the communion ceremony be discontinued, and when the elders of the church did not agree, he resigned.[13]

Resigning as minister of the Second Church, however, did not mean that Emerson ceased preaching. He gave frequent sermons at Unitarian churches in the Boston area. After a sermon in Plymouth in 1834, he was introduced to a young woman named Lydia Jackson, who had previously admired him from afar. She too was a nonconformist Unitarian with Neoplatonist beliefs. Without any formal courtship, Emerson proposed marriage to her by letter in January 1835, and they became engaged a month later. At Emerson's request, she changed her first name to Lydian. The couple was married in July and moved into a house in Concord that Emerson had purchased the previous spring for $3,500.[14] He was offered a pastorate at a Unitarian church in East Lexington, which he declined, but agreed to preach there each Sunday on a temporary basis. The fact that the small village of Lexington could support two Unitarian churches, plus the Congregational church from which they had separated, shows the strength of Unitarianism in Boston and its suburbs.

During the spring of 1836, Emerson began writing what would become one of his best-known works, *Nature*. It was published that same year in September as a small volume of ninety-five pages. (In modern 6" x 9" format, it is only thirty-two pages.) The epigraph on the title page is a quotation from Plotinus, "Nature is but an image or imitation of wisdom, the last thing of the soul; nature being a thing which doth only do, not know." The book is partly a poetic tribute to nature and partly philosophic musings. It contains some beautiful writing, such as:

> Crossing a bare common, in snow puddles, at twilight, under a clouded sky, without having in my thoughts any occurrence of special fortune, I have enjoyed a perfect exhilaration. Almost I fear to think how glad I am. In the

woods, too, a man casts off his years, as the snake his slough, and at what period soever of life, is always a child. In the woods, is perpetual youth.[15]

The philosophy expressed by Emerson in *Nature* is deistic in that it acknowledges a Creator who establishes a world ruled by natural laws. On the other hand, it goes further than deism in defining the creative spirit as still present, though not as a Christian God accessible by prayer. Emerson says, "The currents of the Universal Being circulate through me; I am part or particle of God."[16] This sounds remarkably like the writings of the Stoic Epictetus, quoted in Chapter I.

The French critic Regis Michaud refers to Emerson's *Nature* as "a little manual of pantheism" and says, "For Jehovah, he boldly substitutes Prometheus."[17] Although the book was praised by Emerson's friends and such luminaries as Thomas Carlyle in Scotland, it was disparaged by the American philosophical and religious establishment. Francis Bowen, who taught philosophy at Harvard, criticized "loose and rambling speculations, mystical forms of expression, and the utterance of truths that are but half-perceived."[18]

While Emerson was finishing *Nature,* he had a three-week visit from a twenty-six-year-old woman named Margaret Fuller, who had been anxious to meet him. Fuller was the highly intelligent oldest child of a Boston lawyer, who was a strict taskmaster in educating her. He began teaching her to read and write at age three and a half and started drilling her in Latin from age six.[19] Fuller also studied Greek and decided that the Greek heros were much more attractive than the Biblical figures. At age fifteen she began meeting with a local author, Maria Francis, who guided her in reading such authors as the French thinker Jean Jacques Rousseau and the Stoic Epictetus.[20] Both Emerson and Lydian became fond of her and the three saw each other frequently over the next ten years. Fuller introduced Emerson to such writers as George Sand (the pseudonym used by the French writer Amandine Aurore-Lucie Dudevant) and helped him to understand the German novelist and poet Johann Goethe.[21]

Two years after the publication of *Nature,* Emerson caused an even greater stir with an address to the seniors of Harvard Divinity School on July 15, 1838, the eve of their graduation. In the address he criticized the Unitarian clergy for their stupidity and incompetence, saying that their sermons were based on the Bible rather than on their personal experience of their own "indwelling Supreme Spirit."[22] Professor Andrews Norton of the Harvard Divinity School accused Emerson of following "the celebrated atheist Spinoza, and while claiming to be a Christian, denies Christianity in a denial of its miracles."[23]

It was during that same year, 1838, that Emerson became close to Henry David Thoreau, a fellow resident of Concord to whom he had previously given tickets to some of his lectures. Thoreau, born in Concord in 1817, like Emerson attended Harvard. At Harvard he studied Greek, Latin, French, German, Italian Spanish, and took a three-term sequence in intellectual philosophy.[24] He read widely, especially poetry in his junior and senior years. Among the library books he borrowed was Emerson's *Nature,* which he checked out of the library twice. Thoreau graduated from Harvard in 1837 with an academic record better than Emerson had achieved.[25]

After graduation from Harvard, Thoreau was hired by the village of Concord to teach in its public school. His salary of $500 per year was one of the highest in the system. His public-school teaching career, however, lasted only two weeks. A member of the school committee visited Thoreau's classroom and severely criticized him for not whipping the students to maintain discipline. Thoreau's response was to pick several boys and girls at random from his class, whip them lightly, and resign. After unsuccessfully trying to find another public-school teaching job, he opened his own small academy with four students.[26]

Thoreau continued to read widely. The *Enchiridion* of

EMERSON AND THOREAU

Epictetus, the Roman philosopher of the Stoic school mentioned in Chapter I, appeared on his list of classical reading for 1838-1839. A biographer of Thoreau, Robert D. Richardson, Jr., states, "Thoreau was, like Emerson, importantly indebted to Stoicism."[27]

During this period, Thoreau started taking frequent walks with Emerson, and as their friendship ripened, it culminated with Thoreau moving in with Emerson and his wife to act as the man of the house while Emerson was away on his frequent lecture tours.[28] Thoreau became very fond of Lydian, but biographers of both men agree that Thoreau's love went no further than affection. Thoreau at this point in his life, with Emerson's encouragement, was writing both poetry and essays. A number of these were published in the new transcendentalist journal, *The Dial,* of which Margaret Fuller was the editor. The following paragraph is from an essay by Thoreau titled "The Natural History of Massachusetts" published in *The Dial* in July 1842:

> We fancy that this din of religion, literature, and philosophy, which is heard in pulpits, lyceums, and parlors, vibrates through the universe, and is as catholic a sound as the creaking of the earth's axle; but if a man sleep soundly, he will forget it all between sunset and dawn....When I detect a beauty in any of the recesses of nature, I am reminded, by the serene and retired spirit in which it requires to be contemplated, of the inexpressible privacy of a life—how silent and unambitious it is. The beauty there is in mosses must be considered from the holiest, quietest nook.[29]

Thoreau was able to find this privacy three years later in 1845 when he received permission from Emerson to build a cabin in the woods on a fourteen-acre site on Walden Pond that Emerson had purchased in 1844 for $214.[30] Thoreau's life in this cabin for the next two years and two months was the basis for his book *Walden*. The book went through several drafts before it was finally published in 1854 and has become one of the classics of American literature. The volume captures well the love of nature of the transcendentalists:

> Every morning was a cheerful invitation to make my life of equal simplicity, and I may say innocence, with Nature herself. I have been as sincere a worshiper of Aurora as the Greeks. I got up early and bathed in the pond; that was a religious exercise, and one of the best things which I did. They say that characters were engraven on the bathing tub of King Tching-Thang[a] to this effect: "Renew thyself completely each day; do it again, and again, and forever again." I can understand that. Morning brings back the heroic ages....That man who does not believe that each day contains an earlier, more sacred and auroral hour than he has profaned, has despaired of life and is pursuing a descending and darkening way. After a partial sensation of his sensuous life, the soul of man, or its organs rather, are invigorated each day, and his Genius tries again what noble life it can make. All memorable events, I should say, transpire in morning time and in a morning atmosphere. The Vedas say, "All intelligences awake with the morning."... All poets and heroes, like Memnon, are the children of Aurora, and emit their music at sunrise.[b]
>
> I went to the woods because I wished to live deliberately, to front only the essential facts of life, and see if I could not learn what it had to teach, and not, when I came to die, discover that I had not lived. I did not wish to live what was not life, living is so dear; nor did I wish to

---

[a] Another name for Confucius.
[b] An Egyptian statue of King Amenhotep, sacred to Memnon, son of Aurora, was believed to emit musical notes at sunrise.

practice resignation, unless it was quite necessary. I wanted to live deep and suck out all of the marrow of life, to live so sturdily and Spartan-like as to put to rout all that was not life, to cut a broad swath and shave close, to drive life into a corner, and reduce it to its lowest terms, and if it proved to be mean, why then to get the whole and genuine meanness of it, and publish its meanness to the world; or if it were sublime, to know it by experience, and to be able to give a true account of it in my next excursion.[31]

In the summer of 1846, about half-way through his stay at Walden Pond, Thoreau spent a night in the Concord jail for nonpayment of his poll tax. He later wrote in his essay "Civil Disobedience," "It is for no particular item in the tax bill that I refuse to pay it. I simply wish to refuse allegiance to the State, to withdraw and stand aloof from it effectually."[32] Other writings make it clear that at this time he was particularly concerned with the United States' annexation of Texas and its war with Mexico. The essay also states, "Under a government which imprisons any unjustly, the true place for a just man is also a prison."[33] The philosophy of nonresistance stressed in the essay has influenced generations of peaceful reformers, including Mohandas Gandhi and Martin Luther King, Jr.

After his night in the Concord jail, Thoreau spent another year at Walden, during which time he completed his first draft of *Walden* and his second draft of *A Week on the Concord and Merrimac River*. He also had time to read Homer, Ovid, Cicero, and the Hindu *Bhagavad Gita*. Both Thoreau and Emerson read widely in the Hindu scriptures—not only the *Bhagavad Gita* but also the *Samkhyya Karika* and the *Vishnu Purana*.[34] From these Hindu sources stemmed Emerson's poem "Brahma," of which the first and last verses are:

If the red slayer thinks he slays,

ATHEISTS, AGNOSTICS, AND DEISTS IN AMERICA

> Or if the slain thinks he is slain,
> They know not well the subtle ways
> I keep, and pass, and turn again.
>
> The strong gods pine for my abode,
> And pine in vain the sacred Seven;
> But thou, meek lover of the good!
> Find me, and turn thy back on heaven.[35]

In *Walden* Thoreau states at the end of the paragraph previously quoted, "For most men, it appears to me are in a strange uncertainty about whether [the world] is of the devil or of God and have *somewhat hastily* concluded that it is the chief end of man here to "glorify God and enjoy him forever." Thoreau's skepticism about whether the purpose of life is to "glorify God," his knowledge of Greek, Roman, and Hindu literature and myths, and his glorification of Nature were shared by the other transcendentalists, including the Unitarian minister Theodore Parker.

Parker was born in Lexington in 1810, seven years after Emerson's birth and seven years before Thoreau's. He was the grandson of Captain John Parker, the commander of the Militia at the Lexington Green on April 19, 1776, when the shots were fired that ignited the American Revolution. From the time he was a teenager, Theodore knew that he was headed for the Harvard Divinity School to become a minister, but his family, like Emerson's, could not afford the tuition. Therefore, he taught school in Lexington, Concord, and eventually Boston. By 1834 he had accumulated the resources to enter the Divinity School. He graduated in 1836 and accepted a call to be the minister of the Unitarian church in West Roxbury, a suburb of Boston. That same year he married Lydia Cabot, whom he had met while both were staying at a boarding house in Watertown.[36]

The ministerial position left Parker time for writing. He translated from the German a two-volume work with the title, *A Critical and Historical Introduction to the Canonical Scriptures of the New Testament,* by W.M. De Wette, which has been called "the most important (and most neglected) work of American Biblical scholarship before the Civil War."[37] He also started attending meetings of the Transcendental Club, along with Emerson, Thoreau, Bronson Alcott, George Ripley, and Margaret Fuller.

Parker was one of the sponsors of *The Dial,* the transcendental quarterly launched in 1840 with Fuller as editor, and from the beginning, he was a regular contributor. One of his essays, "A Lesson for the Day, or the Christianity of Christ, of the Church, and of Society," denounced the Christianity of the church as "a very poor thing, a very little better than heathenism."[38] In another *Dial* article, "Thoughts on Labor," Parker wrote, "The present property scheme entails awful evils upon society, rich no less than poor. This question, first of inherited property, and next of all private property, is to be handled in the nineteenth century and made to give its reason why the whole thing should not be abated as a nuisance."[39] This seems to be a forecast of the works of Karl Marx.

Parker's radical ideas on Christianity soon became subjects of his sermons. In an ordination sermon for a young minister at the Hawes Place Church in South Boston, Parker stated that Christianity rests neither on the Gospels nor on the teaching of the Church, nor does it derive added authority from miracles, but rather it rests on "great truths which spring up spontaneous in the holy heart."[40] Soon, most of the Unitarian ministers in the Boston area refused to exchange pulpits with Parker on Sundays. In January 1843, he was called before a meeting of the Boston Association of Ministers, where he was accused of deistic and pantheistic ideas and invited to resign from the association. Parker refused; some friends spoke for him, and the meeting ended amicably.[41] Parker continued to publish articles in *The Dial,* but that journal ceased publication in April 1844.

Largely at Parker's instigation, a new journal, *The*

Massachusetts Quarterly Review, was launched in 1847, with Parker and a young friend of Emerson's, James Cabot, as editors. Emerson was also listed on the masthead, but his principal contribution was an editorial for the opening issue. Contributors included the writer Henry James, the poet James Russell Lowell, the abolitionist Wendell Phillips, and Julia Ward Howe, suffragist and reformer. Almost every issue included an article on some phase of the slavery question.[42]

All of the transcendentalists mentioned in this chapter were active in the abolitionist movement. In 1842 Thoreau, as head of the Concord Lyceum, invited the abolitionist Wendell Phillips to speak. When the Lyceum invited Phillips to speak again in 1844, the curators of the organization resigned in protest, and Emerson and Thoreau were elected in their place.[43] That same year Emerson gave an eloquent address to the Anti-Slavery Society in Concord urging that the United States follow the lead of Great Britain, which had emancipated the slaves in the West Indies in 1834. By 1851 Emerson was speaking out strongly against enforcement of the early fugitive slave law of 1793 requiring the return of fugitive slaves to their owners, a measure which the Boston merchants supported. Parker also vigorously fought the return of fugitive slaves and was part of a small band of men who broke down the door of the Boston jail and attempted to rescue Anthony Burns, a fugitive slave from Virginia. Parker and a fellow Unitarian minister were arrested and tried for participation in the break-in, but were acquitted.[44] The abolitionist cause drew Parker and Emerson together, and Parker dedicated a volume called *Ten Sermons* to Emerson.[45]

When the fiery abolitionist John Brown visited Concord in 1857 and spoke, both Emerson and Thoreau were in the audience, and Emerson invited Brown to spend the night in his home.[46] Brown returned to Concord in May 1859, shortly before his doomed raid on the federal arsenal in Harper's Ferry, Virginia. Thoreau, who did not know about the raid in advance, spoke out in Brown's defense in a speech on "A Plea for Captain John Brown," in which he took the position that although violence was bad, slavery was worse. When Brown was hanged, Thoreau organized a memorial service.[47]

Thoreau himself died on May 6, 1862. A few days before his death, a family friend remarked, "You seem so near the brink of the dark river, that I almost wonder how the opposite shore may appear to you." Thoreau's answer was, "One world at a time."[48] His funeral was held in the Unitarian church, although Thoreau had renounced his membership some years earlier. Emerson gave the funeral address.[49]

Fuller had died in 1850 in a shipwreck off Fire Island along the coast of New York, and Parker had died in 1860, but Emerson lived on another twenty years. As he wrote in his poem "Terminus,"

> It is time to be old,
> To take in sail:—
> The god of bounds,
> Who sets to seas a shore,
> Came to me in his fatal rounds,
> And said: 'No more!'[50]

Emerson died after a short illness on April 27, 1882, and was buried in Sleepy Hollow cemetery on the outskirts of Concord.

CHAPTER VI

COLONEL ROBERT INGERSOLL AND OTHER INFIDELS

In the nineteenth century, when no television, movies or radio existed, many Americans sought both education and amusement through attending public lectures. Speaking on the lecture circuit was also an important source of income for many American public figures from Ralph Waldo Emerson to Mark Twain. In the first half of the nineteenth century, abolitionists such as Fanny Wright, Frederick Douglass, and William Lloyd Gaarrison were prominent on the lecture circuit; after the Civil War, Susan B. Anthony, Elizabeth Cady Stanton, and Lucy Stone toured the town halls speaking for the cause of women's rights. During the second half of the nineteenth century, one of the best-known orators on the lecture circuit was Robert Green Ingersoll, known as "the Pagan Prophet." Because he was the most influential figure in the antireligious movement in the latter half of the nineteenth century, we shall devote most of this chapter to him. We shall, however, also review more briefly the lives of two prominent atheists associated with Ingersoll in several organizations, Elizur Wright and De Robigné Mortimer Bennett.

Robert Ingersoll was born in 1833 in Dresden, New York, to Mary and John Ingersoll. John was a Presbyterian minister who preached two sermons each Sunday and required his children to attend both.[1] Robert's later rebellion against organized religion may have stemmed from these dreary Sundays in his father's church. The family moved frequently, as the Reverend Ingersoll was called to a succession of churches in small towns in Ohio, Illinois, and Wisconsin. Robert went to the public schools in these villages, supplementing formal schooling by reading and memorizing large sections of Shakespeare and the poetry of Scotland's Robert Burns.[2] He also spent one year at an academy in Greenville, Illinois, operated by the Reverend Socrates Smith.

This rather meager education qualified Robert to teach school, and for the next two years he taught in Illinois and Tennessee. He hated teaching, however, and with his brother, Ebenezer Clark Ingersoll (known as Clark), studied law with an attorney in Marion, Illinois. After six months of study, they passed the bar examinations in a ceremony which included the requirement for the new lawyers to supply the examiners and officers of the court with all they could eat and drink at the nearest saloon.[3] The brothers established a law office in Shawnee-town, Illinois, a port on the Ohio River, and then in 1858 moved the office to Peoria. Their business prospered, and the Ingersolls became known for their ability to defend criminals. Because of his speaking skills, Robert was asked in 1860 to give the oration at Peoria's Fourth of July celebration.[4]

During these years, Robert continued his self-education by reading widely, sometimes staying up most of the night to finish a book.[5] On his reading list were works by Epicurus, Zeno, Voltaire, and Tom Paine.[6] From Robert's later lifestyle, it seems likely that Epicurus made more of an impression than Zeno the Stoic. He later stated in his lecture, "Why I Am an Agnostic" that:

> I compared Zeno, Epicurus, and Socrates, three heathen wretches who had never heard of the Old Testament or the Ten Commandments, with Abraham, Isaac, and Jacob, three favorites of Jehovah, and I was depraved enough to think that the Pagans were superior to the Pat-riarchs—and to Jehovah himself.[7]

In 1861 Robert acted as defense attorney for a farmer who had murdered the man in charge of the town animal pound because the official had impounded some of the farmer's stray pigs. During the trial, Ingersoll was invited to dinner at the mansion of Benjamin Parker and met the Parkers' daughter, Eva. It was love at first sight. Robert was surprised and delighted to find the works of Paine and Voltaire in the Parker family library. It turned out that Eva's grandmother, Sarah Buckman Parker, was an atheist, and her parents were devotees of Voltaire and Paine. Eva herself was a deist verging on an atheist. Compatibility in religious views undoubtedly smoothed the courtship, and the couple were married on February 13, 1862.[8]

The previous year, as the Civil War commenced, Robert had been instrumental in raising a regiment for the Illinois Volunteer Cavalry and in December became its commanding officer with the title of Colonel. Nine days after his marriage, Ingersoll's cavalry regiment left for St. Louis, and Eva accompanied him. Later she joined him at the front near Jackson, Tennessee. Ingersoll's regiment was defeated by a Confederate force under Brigadier General Nathan Forrest at a battle near Lexington, Tennessee. Ingersoll was captured when his horse fell while jumping a fence and he was held at a country store with other prisoners. According to a later *New York Times* story, "Gen. Forrest offered to exchange him for a mule to prevent his oratory from demoralizing and leading away the whole Confederate force."[9] Ingersoll was paroled after four days and rejoined his wife in Jackson. He reported back to St. Louis in March and resigned from the service in June.[10] Although he served only one year in the Army, he was thereafter known as Colonel Ingersoll.

Following the Civil War, Ingersoll returned to Peoria with Eva and their two daughters.. During the next decade, he resumed his legal career and dabbled in politics, acting as campaign manager for his brother, Clark, who won election to Congress in 1864. As a prominent lawyer, Robert became a familiar figure in Springfield, the state capitol, and was appointed State Attorney General in 1867. The following year he ran for governor of Illinois but lost the nomination in the Republican state convention. Nevertheless, he was active in the campaign of Ulysses S. Grant for the Presidency. In particular, he spoke on Grant's behalf throughout the state of Maine at the invitation of Representative James G. Blaine and received enthusiastic reports of his oratory by the leading Maine newspapers.[11] Eight years later in 1876, when Blaine was a Republican candidate for President, he chose Ingersoll to make his nominating speech at the Republican convention in Cincinnati. It was a stunning speech and Ingersoll's reference to Blaine as "a plumed knight" stuck with the candidate for the rest of his life. The *Cincinnati Enquirer* reported:

> Men may come and go; flowers may wither, and conventions may shrivel and pass into history.... Blaine may be forgotten and the world may grow stale, but the eloquence of that smooth-faced individual from Peoria will live forever. Let that speech of Ingersoll's be graven in letters of gold (standard value) and then placed inside the rotunda of the national capitol.[12]

Although the presidential nomination eventually went to Rutherford B. Hayes, Ingersoll's nominating speech for Blaine secured for him a national reputation and assured large audiences for his speeches that fall in support of Hayes. In New York City, he spoke at Cooper Union, and *The New York Times* reported, "Col. Ingersoll's address was one of the best political speeches ever delivered in New York. It was a bold, logical, eloquent, and fair statement of the political situation....He spoke for nearly two hours and held the complete attention of his audience from beginning to end."[13] The following week when Ingersoll returned to Cincinnati, *The New York Times* headed its dispatch, "AN IMMENSE AUDIENCE ASSEMBLED TO HEAR THE BRILLIANT SPEAKER—SPARKLING WIT, SHARP RETORT AND UNANSWERABLE ARGUMENT AGAINST THE DEMOCRATIC PARTY AND THEIR CANDIDATE."[14]

Ingersoll's reputation as an orator also assured him large audiences for his later antireligious lectures. Following his loss of the nomination for governor of Illinois in 1868, he had started to lecture locally on anticlerical themes. His subjects included "Thomas Paine" in 1871, "The Gods" in 1872, and "Heretics and Heresies" in 1874. Thus, when after the Republican convention, the requests poured in for his services as a lecturer, Ingersoll was well prepared.

Further, by the late 1870s, audiences were tolerant of religious ideas that would have been rejected outright in the 1860s. In part, this was because of the increasing acceptance of scientific explanations for phenomena that had once been explainable only in religious terms. In particular, Darwin's ideas on the origin of species sharply conflicted with the Bible. Further, as James Turner points out in his book *Without God, Without Creed,* many religious leaders made the mistake of trying to adopt religious beliefs to human understanding and aspirations, rather than continuing to teach a transcendent Deity incomprehensible on human terms.[15]

Thus, following the "Plumed Knight" speech, Ingersoll cut back on his law practice and arranged an 1877 transcontinental lecture tour, largely on subjects related to his views on religion, such as those mentioned above. He negotiated his own lecture contracts and prepared the advertising materials, but he did have an advance agent who checked the arrangements along the proposed itinerary. While on tour, he lectured at least three times a week, with fees ranging from $200 to $2,400 for each appearance. (In later years, his fees were as high as $7,000.) He stipulated that the admission fee should be at least fifty cents and was willing to accept either a flat fee or a percentage of gross receipts.[16] A three-month tour would yield an income of more than $30,000. Considering price inflation, this is equivalent to approximately $600,000 in today's dollars.

Ingersoll's tour took him from Illinois west to California by way of Nebraska, Kansas, Colorado, Wyoming, and Nevada. He stayed six weeks in California and then retraced his steps, using a different lecture, and traveled on to New York and the New

England states. His appearance at this time was described in one newspaper as follows:

> He is in the full prime and vigor of life, with a ruddy complexion, a keen sparkling eye, broad, high forehead, made higher by partial baldness, a smooth shaven face, and open, frank countenance.[17]

The comment on Ingersoll's "smooth shaven face" highlights one of his distinguishing features. In a sea of beards which adorned the faces of most public men such as Lincoln and Grant, Ingersoll's clean shaven chin and cheeks were striking.

As for his oratorical ability, Henry Ward Beecher, a Congregational clergyman who was himself internationally known as an excellent speaker, said during a political rally in which both men participated, "I now introduce you to a man who—and I say it not flatteringly—is the most brilliant speaker of the English tongue of all men on this globe."[18]

Ingersoll's most popular lectures were those on science and religion. The Greek philosopher Epicurus, who taught that the principal aim of life should be pleasure (see Chapter I), had a strong influence on Ingersoll, as shown in the first and third of the following excerpts:

> ON THE GODS
> Reason, Observation, and Experience—the Holy Trinity of Science—have taught us that happiness is the only good, that the time to be happy is now, and the way to be happy is to make others so. This is enough for us. In this belief we are content to live and die. If by any possibility the existence of a power superior to, and independent of, nature shall be demonstrated, there will be time enough to kneel. Until then let us stand erect.[19]

ATHEISTS, AGNOSTICS, AND DEISTS IN AMERICA

INDIVIDUALITY

Some throw away the Old Testament and cling to the New, while others give up everything except the idea that there is s personal God, and that in some wonderful way we are the objects of His care. Even this... as Science, the great iconoclast, marches onward, will have to be abandoned with the rest. The great ghost will surely share the fate of the little ones. They fled at the first appearance of the dawn, and the other will vanish with the perfect day.[20]

THE GHOSTS

Happiness is the only possible good, and all that tends to the happiness of man is right, and is of value. All that tends to develop the bodies and minds of men; all that gives us better houses, better clothes, better food, better pictures, grander music, better heads, better hearts; all that renders us more intellectual and more loving, nearer just; that makes us better husbands and wives, better children, better citizens—all these things combine to produce what I call Progress. [21]

I attack the monsters, the phantoms of the imagination that have ruled the world....They blinded the eyes and stopped the ears of the human race. They subverted all ideas of justice by promising infinite rewards for finite virtues and threatening infinite punishment for finite offenses. They filled the future with heavens and with hells, with the shining peaks of selfish joy and the lurid abysses of flames....Man is greater than these phantoms. Humanity is grander than all these creeds. Humanity is the great sea, and these creeds, and books, and religions, are but the waves of a day. Humanity is the sky, and these religions and dogmas and theories are but the mists and clouds, changing continually, destined finally to melt away....Let the ghosts go. We will worship them no more.

ROBERT INGERSOLL AND OTHER INFIDELS

Let them cover their eyeless sockets with their fleshless hands and fade forever from the imaginations of men.

In his lectures and interviews with reporters, Ingersoll usually identified himself as an agnostic, the term was invented by the English philosopher Thomas Huxley in 1869. Later, the idea that there were limits to our knowledge was taken up by Herbert Spencer, another English philosopher. Spencer wrote that the subject matter of religion passes beyond the sphere of experience and that God was not only unknown but unknowable. Huxley and Spencer's philosophy was quickly transplanted to America. The religious historian Sidney Warren places atheism on the left wing of the antireligious movement, agnosticism in the center, and deism in the right wing.[22] Ingersoll wrote about his agnostic views as follows:

> Let us be honest with ourselves. In the presence of countless mysteries, standing beneath the boundless heaven sown thick with constellations; knowing that each grain of sand, each leaf, each blade of grass, asks of every mind the answerless question; knowing that the simplest thing defies solution; feeling that we deal with the superficial and the relative; and that we are forever eluded by the real, the absolute, let us admit the limitations of our minds, and let us have the courage and the candor to say: We do not know.[23]

Following his 1877 lecture tour, Ingersoll moved with his family to Washington, D.C., where he formed a partnership with his brother Clark, who died two years later. Carrying on the practice, Ingersoll acted as defense lawyer for many high-profile cases. One of the most notorious involved officials of the U.S. Post Office who were indicted for defrauding the government in the awarding of contracts for "star routes," which were operated by private concerns under government contract to take mail service to parts of the country without railroad connections. Postal officials were alleged to have conspired to increase the amounts of contracts on twenty-six of these routes from $65,216 to $530,318. Two trials were required because an attempt was made to bribe jurors in the first trial. At the completion of the second trial in 1883, Ingersoll's closing statement took six days. The jury took only two days to reach a verdict of not guilty for all of the defendants.[24]

In addition to his activities as a trial lawyer and his speaking engagements, Ingersoll was also active in the National Liberal League. The league was formed to promote the total separation of church and state, as well as other causes such as women's suffrage and sexual freedom. Ingersoll was made a vice president at the organizational meeting in Philadelphia in 1876. The president was Francis Abbot, a former Unitarian minister. Other vice presidents included Robert Dale Owen, whom we met in Chapter IV, and Elizur Wright, an abolitionist and atheist.

As was the case of several other nonbelievers described in this book, Wright, who was born in 1804 to a strongly Christian family, decided to enter the Christian ministry. He worked his way through Yale, graduating in 1826, but chose to teach at the local academy in Groton, Massachusetts (now Lawrence Academy), rather than immediately entering the ministry.[25] At the academy, he fell in love with one of his students, sixteen-year-old Susan Clark. Two years of teaching school, however, convinced him that he did not wish to pursue a career in education, and he took a job with the American Tract Society to distribute religious tracts in the American West, essentially acting as a lay missionary. He was given the territory of western Pennsylvania at a salary of $150 per year. Wright lasted only four months in this position. He resigned and married Susan, even though she had never met his parents—an example of the independence that he exhibited throughout his adult life. He now needed a job and, fortunately, in 1829 he was appointed a professor of mathematics at Western Reserve College in Ohio.[26]

ROBERT INGERSOLL AND OTHER INFIDELS

During the following years, Wright became an ardent abolitionist. In 1832 he helped found an abolitionist society at Western Reserve College. The following year he moved his family to New York City and became the full-time administrator of the New York headquarters of the American Anti-Slavery Society. His strong feelings in favor of the immediate abolition of slavery led to his disillusionment with the Christian church because most denominations did not share these views. Robert Ingersoll later described Wright's loss of Christian faith as follows:

> He found that a majority of Christians were willing to enslave men and women for whom they said Christ had died....Elizur Wright said to himself, why should we take chains from bodies and enslave minds—why fight to free the cage and leave the bird a prisoner? He became an enemy of orthodox religion—that is to say, a friend of intellectual liberty.[27]

Thus, in the period after the Civil War, many of the former abolitionists banded together to form the National Liberal League mentioned above. At its 1878 meeting, the principal item on the agenda was discussion of the Comstock laws.. These laws outlawed the use of the U.S. mails for transmission of obscene material, including erotic literature, birth control information, and atheistic tracts.[28] At the time of the meeting, attention was focused on the arrest under the Comstock laws of two men—De Robigné Mortimer Bennett, a publisher, and Ezra Hervey Heywood, an author. Heywood's offense was to write a pamphlet titled *Cupid's Yokes: or the Binding Forces of Conjugal Life*, which advocated free love. Since Heywood's interest was in sex, rather than religion, he is only peripherally related to this book. Bennett, however, was an influential atheist and, like Ingersoll and Wright, a vice president of the Liberal League.[29]

Bennett was born on December 23, 1818, to Methodist parents on a farm near Otsego Lake in Springfield, New York. At age fourteen he left home and joined a Shaker colony in New Lebanon, New York, where he learned herbal medicine and became the community's physician. Bennett also met his future wife, Mary Wicks, at the New Lebanon colony. When he left the Shakers in 1846, he used his medicinal skills to manufacture and sell Dr. Bennett's Quick Cure, Golden Liniment, Worm Lozenges, and Root and Plant Pills. During this period of his life, he read Thomas Paine's *Age of Reason* and became an atheist. Eventually he moved to Paris, Illinois, where he operated a seed business. Because the local paper would not publish his comments on sermons by a Paris preacher, Bennett founded his own atheistic periodical, the *Truth Seeker*. In December of 1873, he moved to New York City, taking the newspaper with him. He published excepts from the *Truth Seeker* as pamphlets, as well various other liberal materials. In addition to publishing, Bennett lectured on antireligious themes.[30] In 1877 he was arrested by a U.S. marshall in the company of Anthony Comstock on a charge of sending obscene matter through the mails. The "obscene matter" consisted of a pamphlet written by Bennett called *An Open Letter to Jesus Christ* and a scientific treatise titled *How Do Marsupials Propagate Their Kind?* Bennett had to post a $1500 bail bond, but Robert Ingersoll brought the matter to the attention of the Postmaster General in Washington, and the case was eventually dismissed.[31]

Bennett was not deterred. He inserted a notice in the *Truth Seeker* that he was willing to send the pamphlet *Cupid's Yokes*, referred to above, to anybody who wanted it. Comstock ordered the pamphlet under an assumed name, and when it arrived through the mail, Bennett was again arrested. This time he was tried and found guilty. The National Liberal League led a campaign for his pardon by President Rutherford B. Hayes, but an even stronger campaign directed by the religious community at Hayes' wife, a strong Methodist, led the President to turn down the pardon appeals. Bennett was sent to the Albany Penitentiary for thirteen months of hard labor. He was released in August

ROBERT INGERSOLL AND OTHER INFIDELS

1880, and his friends celebrated by giving him a large reception at Chickering Hall in New York City. After his release, Bennett traveled to Europe as a delegate to a conference of freethinkers, but his prison experience had adversely affected his health, and he died in December 1882. Bennett's monument was inscribed, "The Defender of Liberty and Its Martyr."[32]

During this period, the National Liberal League was divided over the question as to whether or not to press for repeal of the Comstock Laws. Ingersoll advocated amendment of the laws, rather than repeal, At the 1879 meeting of the League in Cincinnati, a resolution was passed stating

> We are utterly opposed to the dissemination through the mails, or by any other means, of obscene literature, whether "inspired" or uninspired; we call upon the Christian world to expunge from the so-called "sacred" Bible every passage that cannot be read without covering the cheek of modesty with the blush of shame, and until such passages are expunged, we demand that the laws against dissemination of obscene literature be impartially enforced; that we are in favor of such postal laws as will allow the free transportation through the mails of the United States of all books, pamphlets, and papers irrespective of the religious, irreligious, political, and scientific views they may contain, so that the literature of science may be placed upon an equality with that of superstition.[33]

This wording pleased both those advocating repeal of the laws and those seeking amendment. At the meeting of the league in Chicago in 1880, though, those advocating outright repeal passed a resolution to that effect, and Ingersoll resigned. Wright continued as president until the league dissolved in 1884 in favor of a new society, the American Secular Union, this time with Ingersoll as president. The new organization favored taxation of church property, elimination of chaplains from the armed services and from Congress, and abandonment of religious teaching in the public schools.[34] Wright died the following year, 1885, and that same year Ingersoll resigned as president of the American Secular Union, feeling he was more effective as an individual lecturer than as part of an organization.

In 1885, Ingersoll and his family moved to New York City, where they lived first on Fifth Avenue and then on Grammercy Park. He established his law offices on Wall Street and enjoyed New York's theatrical and musical life. When his daughter Eva married a wealthy railroad magnate, Walston Hill Brown, Ingersoll agreed with his new son-in-law that the two families would live together, spending winters at Ingersoll's home on Grammercy Park and summers at Brown's castle in Dobbs Ferry, New York. In spite of this unorthodox arrangement, Eva's marriage turned out to be a long and happy one.

In addition to working for religious freedom, Ingersoll supported many other liberal causes, including women's suffrage, equal rights for blacks, and unrestricted immigration.[35] He supported the candidacy for mayor of New York City of Henry George, the author of *Progress and Poverty*, a book that sold more copies than any other work on economics. Urging a single tax on land to replace all other taxes, George out-polled Theodore Roosevelt, the Republican candidate for mayor, but lost to the Democrat, Abram Hewitt.[36]

Ingersoll also continued to lecture. One of his most controversial lectures, "A Christmas Sermon," was printed in the New York *Evening Telegram* on December 19, 1891. In it, Ingersoll maintained that Christmas was originally a pagan festival celebrating the triumph of the sun god over the powers of darkness at the time of the winter solstice. He then went on to condemn Christianity. "It has filled the future with fear and flame, and made God the keeper of an eternal penitentiary, destined to be the home of nearly all the sons of men." The *Telegram* was flooded with letters, and its circulation soared.

Another controversy arose in 1895 when Ingersoll was

scheduled to lecture in Hoboken, New Jersey. A group of local ministers resurrected a New Jersey statute against blasphemy and convinced the mayor to deny Ingersoll the use of the opera house. Ingersoll and his manager appealed this decision to the city attorney, who ruled that he could speak under the New Jersey constitution free-speech clause, but that he was subject to prosecution under the blasphemy statute if he violated it. In the lecture, Ingersoll cleverly evaded the letter of the law by prefacing potentially blasphemous remarks with statements such as, "I don't know. If it weren't for the Jersey statutes, I might know."[37]

Ingersoll was the object of many efforts to convert him to Christianity. In Cleveland, the Christian Endeavor Union resolved that each of its three-thousand members should pray for his conversion at noon on Thanksgiving Day, 1895. This mass prayer inspired members of Christian Endeavor groups in other cities in the United States and Canada. Ingersoll's reaction was that this was progress, since at one time they would have burned him rather than pray for him. [38]

Ingersoll continued to lecture until June, 1899, a month before he died. In his last lecture, titled "What is Religion," he asked:

Has man obtained any help from Heaven? Can we affect the nature and qualities of substance by prayer? Can we hasten or delay the tides by worship? Can we change winds by sacrifice? Will kneeling give us wealth?...Is there any evidence for a *yes* to these questions?[39]

In the report of his death on July 21, 1899, at his son-in-law's home, Walton, in Dobbs Ferry, *the New York Times* reported:

Col. Ingersoll is believed to have died without any modification of his unbelief in the teachings of the Bible. He called himself a consistent agnostic and said he could not believe anything unless it could be demonstrated. As late as last Sunday in a conversation with two or three friends at Walton, he expressed himself regarding Christianity in the same spirit and tone that have made him the most noted of English-speaking infidels.[40]

Ingersoll continued to be influential after his death, both through ongoing readership of his books, through young people he had influenced, and through the organizations with which he was associated. The American Secular Union, of which Ingersoll had served as the first president, initially prospered after his death. According to the *Truth Seeker*, by 1900 it had forty to fifty-thousand members. From that point on, however, the organization declined and disappeared from the pages of the *Truth Seeker* after 1910.[41]

Among those whom Ingersoll influenced both as an orator and as an agnostic was the lawyer Clarence Darrow. We shall review his life and influence in the next chapter.

CHAPTER VII

THE LAST OF THE ATHEIST ORATORS— CLARENCE DARROW

Of those in the next generation influenced by Robert Ingersoll, probably the best known is the lawyer Clarence Darrow. As a young man, Darrow heard Ingersoll speak and tried to adopt his style of oratory. He found, however, that he was not comfortable in imitating Ingersoll and went back to his normal way of expression.[1] At a memorial service to Ingersoll in 1900, Darrow said, "I pay homage to Robert G. Ingersoll....His acts mark him as one of the bravest, grandest champions of human liberty the world has ever seen."[2]

Darrow was born on April 18, 1857 in the small town of Kinsman, Ohio, about ten miles west of Meadsville, Pennsylvania. His father had graduated from the Unitarian seminary in Meadsville, where he had read Emerson and Theodore Parker but soon lost all faith in even the liberal Unitarian beliefs. Both Darrow's father and mother were readers of Jefferson, Voltaire, and Paine.[3] Since Darrow specifically mentions these authors in his autobiography, it is likely that he read them also. After high school, Darrow spent one year at Allegheny college in Meadsville, but a financial panic in 1873 made it impossible for his parents to continue to pay tuition. Accordingly he worked at a local factory in the summer and taught school in the winter until he had saved up enough money for a year at the University of Michigan Law School. Although the course was for two years, he left after one year and entered a law office in Youngstown, Ohio, as a student clerk. With this rather sketchy training, Darrow managed to pass the bar exams in 1878 at the age of twenty-one.[4] Two years later he married Jessie Ohl, the daughter of the owner of the local grist mill, and attempted to set up a law practice in Andover, another small town in Ohio near the Pennsylvania border. In Andover, however, he found that income from defending farmers from charges of watering their milk or settling disputes over ownership of harnesses for horses was insufficient to support himself and Jessie. Accordingly, he moved to the larger town of Ashtabula, Ohio, where his law practice prospered. While living in Ashtabula, he was given two books by friends that would influence his life—Henry George's *Progress and Poverty* and *Our Penal Code and Its Victims* by Judge John P. Altgeld.

We mentioned Henry George in the previous chapter in connection with Ingersoll's interest in George's single-tax plan and his support of George in his mayoral race in New York City. George's analysis in *Progress and Poverty* of the destructive effects on society and democracy of the gross inequality of wealth and income distribution immediately attracted the idealistic Darrow. When he moved to Chicago from Ashtabula in 1888, Darrow sought out Judge Altgeld, an important member of the Illinois Democratic Party who was in a position to help him.[5] Darrow also soon joined the Henry George Single Tax Club, and he achieved sufficient recognition so that when Henry George came to Chicago to speak in the city's largest auditorium, Darrow was selected to follow him on the program. He was warmly applauded and the speech was favorably reported in the Chicago newspapers. As a result of this speech, which was attended by the Chicago mayor, Darrow was asked to be an attorney in the city's law office.[6] With the behind-the-scenes help of Altgeld, he soon rose to be corporation counsel, in charge of all of the city's lawyers. Continuing in this position for three years, Darrow was well started on his career.

This career encompassed acting as defense attorney in some of the most famous cases in the United States during the first quarter of the twentieth century, including the defense of Richard Loeb and Nathan Leopold, Jr. for the kidnaping and murder of a fourteen-year-old Chicago boy and the trial of "Big

CLARENCE DARROW

Bill" Haywood, the general secretary of the Western Federation of Miners, on the charge of conspiring in the murder of the former governor of Idaho, Frank Steunenberg . In this chapter, we shall concentrate on two cases early and late in Darrow's career as a lawyer—the defense of Eugene V. Debs in connection with his arrest in the 1894 strike of workers against the Pullman Company and the defense of John T. Scopes in his trial for violation of Tennessee's statute against teaching the theory of evolution in the public schools.

The Pullman case arose out of a labor dispute at the Pullman Company near Chicago, Illinois. George Pullman had invented the modern railroad sleeping car and risked his life savings to build it. The company was very successful, and Pullman built what was regarded as a model town to house its workers. As a condition of employment, workmen were required to rent company houses at a rental established by the company, with the rent deducted from their pay checks. All was well until a financial panic in 1893 cut into Pullman's sales and profits. The solution for Pullman was to switch from hourly pay, which had averaged $3.20 per day, to piece work, which produced income of only $1.20 per day. Rents were not decreased, so most workers received a net pay of $1.00 or less every two weeks to cover costs for food and other expenses for their families. With their families starving, the men organized a union and asked to open negotiations, providing the company would not discharge the union delegates. A vice president did sit down with the workers but the next morning all of the union delegates were fired and evicted from their homes. The union then went on strike on May 11, 1894, and Pullman responded by laying off all remaining workers and closing the shops. By coincidence, the American Railway Union (ARU) held its convention in Chicago three weeks later and unanimously agreed to a motion that no ARU member should handle trains to which Pullman cars were attached.[7] The ARU's effort was led by Eugene V. Debs.

Debs was born in 1855 in Terre Haute, Indiana, where his

97

parents ran a small grocery store. As he grew up, his father, who with his mother had emigrated from Alsace in 1849, read the children the French classics, including Voltaire and other Enlightenment writers.[8] Eugene attended both private and public schools but left school at age fifteen to go to work as a paint scraper for a local railroad. Although he temporarily left railroading for a job as an accounting clerk, he attended the organizational meeting of the Brotherhood of Locomotive Firemen in Terre Haute in 1875. He was elected recording secretary, but continued to work in the grocery business. He then entered politics, first as the city clerk and then as a representative to the state assembly. At the same time, he advanced in his union and became secretary-treasurer of the national brotherhood and editor of its journal.

Debs' increasing involvement with the labor movement also changed his religious views. He distanced himself from organized religion, claiming that the American churches of all denominations had a strong antilabor bias. Although not an atheist, Debs never joined a church. Like Darrow, he also supported the single-tax proposals of Henry George.[9]

In 1893 Debs helped found the new American Railway Union, which combined the various brotherhoods, and led a successful strike against the Great Northern Railway the following year. Thus, at the time of the Pullman strike, Debs was a nationally known labor leader.

After the American Railway Union resolution refusing to handle trains with Pullman cars, the conflict escalated. Although today lawyers agree that the federal government can send troops into a state only at the request of the state legislature or governor, President Grover Cleveland sent federal troops to Chicago at the request of a special U.S. attorney with connections to the railway companies.[10] At the same time, Debs and his fellow union officers were enjoined in federal court to call off the strike. They were also charged by a federal grand jury with conspiracy. It was at this point that the union asked Darrow to help them, and he agreed to do so on a *pro bono* (no fee) basis.

In his autobiography, Darrow wrote that at the time he took the case, "I believed that the distribution of wealth was grossly unjust, and I sympathized with almost all efforts to get higher wages and to improve general conditions of the masses."[11]
This belief was in accordance with his general view of man's place in the universe:

> All that we know is that we were born on this little grain of sand we call earth....The best that we can do is to be kindly and helpful to our friends and fellow passengers who are clinging to the same speck of dirt while we are drifting side by side to our fellow doom.[12]

The conspiracy case was brought to court first in a trial by jury, during which Darrow made a brilliant defense both in his arguments for the accused and in his cross-examination of prosecution witnesses. It seemed obvious that Darrow was winning. When one juror fell ill, the judge adjourned the case, and it was never resumed. In the civil case involving the injunction, though, Darrow was only one of three lawyers conducting the defense. The judge heard the arguments and ruled that the union had acted in restraint of trade under the Sherman Act. Debs and his fellow unionists were sentenced to six months in jail.

Debs continued to work on union affairs from his jail cell. He also later wrote that it was this jail experience which led him to become a Socialist.[13] He ran for the Presidency on the Socialist ticket in 1912, receiving nearly 900,000 votes, and was imprisoned again n 1918 for his pacifist views during World War I. As was the case with D.M. Bennett, who was imprisoned for his atheistic views, Debs' health was adversely affected by his prison life, and he died in 1926. Darrow wrote in his autobiography, "There may have lived some time, some where, a kindlier, gentler, more generous man than Eugene V. Debs, but I have never known him."[14]

ATHEISTS, AGNOSTICS, AND DEISTS IN AMERICA

Although the Pullman case made Darrow famous, it provided little opportunity for him to express his religious beliefs. The prosecution in Dayton, Tennessee, of John T. Scopes, a Dayton public school teacher, for teaching the Darwinian theory of evolution, on the other hand, involved a direct conflict between atheism/agnosticism and Christian fundamentalist beliefs in the literal accuracy of the Bible as a historical record of Creation. William Jennings Bryan, the lawyer for the prosecution, was a three-time Presidential candidate, the leader of the Democratic Party, and the Secretary of State under President Woodrow Wilson. He also was a fundamentalist and largely responsible for the laws in Tennessee and other southern states making it illegal to teach the theory of evolution in public schools. Even though he had not practiced law for thirty-six years, Bryan volunteered to head up the prosecution of Scopes.[15] He announced before the trial, "A successful attack would destroy the Bible and with it revealed religion. If evolution wins, Christianity goes." Darrow also volunteered to act as counsel for the defense without fee.[16]

Before continuing with the Scopes trial, we shall digress briefly to examine the influence of Charles Darwin on religion in America. Darwin was born in 1809 in Shrewsbury, England. He grew up in a family of orthodox members of the Church of England and spent three years at Cambridge University in preparation for a career as a clergyman. At age 22, however, he received an appointment as an unpaid naturalist on a naval surveying expedition. During his voyage on the government research ship *Beagle* from 1831 to 1836, he amassed a large number of observations of animals and plants, especially noting the differences in species isolated from one another on remote islands. After his return to England, Darwin analyzed his data and hit upon his theory of natural selection—that favorable variations in individual members of a species would tend to be preserved and unfavorable ones destroyed. In 1856 when he found that a fellow biologist, Alfred Wallace, had reached the same conclusion and was about to publish an article on the subject, Darwin arranged for the two men to present their papers at the same meeting of the Linnean Society. In 1859, Darwin published his best-known work, *Origin of Species,* followed in 1871 by *The Descent of Man.*

Although by the time he wrote *Origin of Species* Darwin had lost his faith in Christianity, he continued to be a theist, as shown in this passage from his autobiography:

> Another source of conviction in the existence of God...follows from the extreme difficulty, or rather impossibility of conceiving this immense and wonderful universe, including man with his capacity of looking far backwards and far into futurity, as the result of blind chance or necessity. When thus reflecting, I felt compelled to look to a First Cause having an intelligence in some degree analogous to that of man; and I deserve to be called a Theist[17].

In his latter years, though, Darwin became an agnostic. Further, in his book *The Descent of Man,* Darwin specifically rejected the theory that the general belief in God was genetically based, or in his words "aboriginally endowed," as follows:

> There is no evidence that man was aboriginally endowed with the ennobling belief in the existence of an Omnipotent God. On the contrary, there is ample evidence, derived not from hasty travelers, but from men who have long resided with savages, that numerous races have existed, and still exist who have no idea of one or more gods, and have no words in their language to express such an idea.... If, however, we include under the term "religion" the belief in unseen or spiritual agencies, the case is wholly different; for this belief seems to be universal with the less civilized races....It is also probable that dreams may have first given rise to the notion of spirits; for

savages do not readily distinguish between subjective and objective impressions.[18]

Darwin's theory of natural selection and the evolution of species was immediately challenged by the religious establishment both in Great Britain and in America. Even 140 years after the publication in 1859 of *Origin of Species,* the religious right still clings to the Biblical account of creation.

Now to return to Darrow and Scopes. The town of Dayton, where the Scopes trial took place, quickly assumed a circus-like atmosphere. One man who had brought two chimpanzees to testify for the prosecution rented a store and set them up for a sideshow. Hot-dog stands and lemonade stands lined the streets and the town was inundated with photographers, newspapermen, radio reporters, and telegraph operators.[19] Bryan arrived in Dayton several days before the trial, and in a speech to the Progressive Dayton Club, he pledged that if the verdict in the trial went against him, he would work to amend the Constitution to prohibit the teaching of evolution.[20]

The trial was conducted before twelve farmers, one of whom was illiterate[21] The trial was opened with a prayer by a fundamentalist minister, to which Darrow objected. The judge compromised by opening court the next day with a prayer by the Reverend Charles Potter, a Unitarian minister from New York City, who was present as a defense witness. The prosecution objected to the Unitarian prayer, whereupon the judge announced:

The Court in selecting ministers to open the Court with prayer has had no regard to denominational lines and no concern about sects. The Court believes that any religious society that is worthy of the name should believe in God and believe in divine guidance. The Court has not purposed by opening the court with prayer to influence anyone wrongfully. I do not see how it can do anybody any harm, and it may do some good.[22]

The New York Times reported that in saying, "it may do some good," the judge looked directly at Darrow. When the trial continued, the judge ruled that the scientific evidence for evolution could not be presented to the jury, since the issue was only whether Scopes had taught the subject in defiance of Tennessee law, not whether it was scientifically correct. An angry Darrow threatened to take the case to some other court and dared the judge to cite him for contempt. The judge obliged, setting Darrow's bail at $5,000. Darrow later apologized and the judge forgave him.[23]

The following week the judge moved the trial out to the courthouse lawn to provide room for more spectators. Darrow demanded that the large sign on the courthouse wall urging READ YOUR BIBLE be removed, and the judge agreed.[24] The defense called Bryan as a witness and proceeded to grill him on his beliefs in the literal truth of the Bible, including questions on Jonah and the whale, Joshua and the sun, where Cain got his wife, the date of the flood, and the Tower of Babel. When asked by the prosecuting attorney about the "meaning of all this harangue," Darrow replied, "To show up Fundamentalism; to prevent bigots and ignoramuses from controlling the educational system of the United States." At this, Bryan sprang to his feet and said that he was trying "to protect the Word of God from the greatest atheist and agnostic in the United States."[25] The following morning, the judge cut off further testimony by Bryan as irrelevant and expunged the previous day's testimony from the record. Darrow had anticipated this move and had decided not to argue for a not-guilty verdict for Scopes. Under Tennessee law, this maneuver deprived Bryan of the opportunity to make a closing statement. The jury quickly found Scopes guilty. The judge fined Scopes $100 and closed the trial with a benediction by a minister.

Both Bryan and Darrow made short speeches after the close of the formal trial proceedings. Darrow said

> I think this case will be remembered because it is the first case of this sort since we stopped trying people in America for witchcraft, because here we have done our best to turn back the tide that has sought to force itself upon this modern world of testing every fact in science by a religious dictum.[26]

During the course of the trial, Darrow had won the respect of the community, and after the court was over, many people crowded around him to express their thanks for his defense of Scopes and to say that they were ashamed of Tennessee's anti-evolution law.[27] The case was appealed to the Supreme Court of Tennessee, which reversed the decision because the court rather than the jury had fixed the fine. It also dismissed the case.[28] The issue of the teaching of evolution in the public schools was finally settled in 1968 when the United States Supreme Court ruled that at Arkansas statute forbidding the teaching of Darwin's theory of evolution was unconstitutional because it violated the establishment of religion clause in the Constitution.[29]

With the fame resulting from the Scopes trial, Darrow decided to retire from the rigorous life of a defense attorney and go on the lecture circuit. He found a lecture manager, George Whitehead, who arranged for Darrow to speak in four-way debates with a Catholic priest, a Protestant clergyman, and a Jewish rabbi. These debates were extremely popular. Once in Pittsburgh a thousand people who had been unable to secure tickets staged a near riot to get in, necessitating police interference to control the mob. The entertainment magazine *Variety* described Darrow as America's greatest one-man stage draw.[30]

During the years 1930-1931, Darrow also completed his autobiography, *The Story of My Life*. In addition to biographical material, the book contains a number of chapters expressing his religious and philosophical views. In the chapter "Questions without Answers," he asks, "If God made the Universe, what did he make it of? Did he make it out of nothing?"[31] In the chapter "Future Life," Darrow states, "There is no evidence of mind or personality existing outside of or apart from a physical form."[32] "Delusion of Design and Purpose" points out that many parts of the human body, including the eye, "are botch work that any good mechanic would be ashamed to make."[33] These points of view furnished ample material for his debates with the Protestant, Catholic, and Jewish clergymen.

It is not clear how many people Darwin converted from the traditional religious beliefs to his agnosticism/atheism. There is no question that his beliefs appealed to college students, and some undoubtedly did leave their families' churches. Further, the Scopes trial served as a rallying point for those who were already agnostics and atheists. As we shall see in the next chapters, the era between World War I and the Great Depression was one of significant growth of the nonorthodox movements, and Darrow undoubtedly contributed to this.

Darrow died in March 1938 after a long mental and physical decline. He had asked a friend, Judge William H. Holly, to speak at his memorial service and Judge Holly chose to deliver the same funeral oration that Darrow had given forty years before at the grave of his old patron, Judge Altgeld. So Darrow, in a sense, wrote his own funeral speech . It concluded, "But though we lay you in the grave and hide you from the sight of man, your brave words will speak for the poor, the oppressed, the captive, and the weak, and your devoted life will inspire countless souls to do and dare in the holy cause for which you lived and died."

Darrow was the last of the chain of charismatic speakers on atheism/agnosticism who toured the country giving lectures. We have seen in previous chapters how popular Fannie Wright, Robert Owen, Ralph Waldo Emerson, and Robert Ingersoll toured the lecture circuit. Each of them gave essentially a series of set speeches before a succession of audiences. People attended the lectures in part for the thrill of being shocked by heretical views. With the coming of radio and later television, the audience for this kind of intellectual entertainment moved from the lecture hall to the home. For some reason, most people on the receiving end of the one-on-one communication of television and radio feel more comfortable hearing a preacher expound familiar beliefs rather than listening to outrageous statements by someone like Ingersoll or Darrow.

None of the orators mentioned in the previous paragraph founded enduring organizations to perpetuate their beliefs. A number of organizations of freethinkers, though, were formed in the late nineteenth and early twentieth centuries, and the remainder of the book will be devoted to their history.

CHAPTER VIII

UNITARIANS, UNIVERSALISTS, AND THE FREE RELIGIOUS ASSOCIATION

With this chapter, the book shifts its focus from influential nonbelievers, such as Clarence Darrow, to organizations whose membership now includes deists and atheists. The largest of the liberal religious groups in America at the end of the nineteenth century were the Unitarians and the Universalists, who merged their denominations in May 1961 to become the Unitarian Universalist Association, informally known as the UUs. At the time of their merger, they had slightly under 200,000 members. During the 1970s, membership declined but by 1998 had risen back to 204,000.[1] Although small compared with Roman Catholics (60 million) or Southern Baptists (15 million), the UUs are still a significant force in American society.[2] Further, as we shall see, about half of the UUs hold atheistic views and thus account for the largest group of organized atheists in the country.

As their name implies, the Unitarians rejected the doctrine of the Trinity in favor of belief in a single divinity. In New England during the late eighteenth century and the early part of the nineteenth century, theological debates in the Congregational churches between those endorsing orthodox Trinitarian views and parishioners taking the Unitarian position split many congregations. The situation was complicated by the relation between church and state in Massachusetts. Unlike the federal Constitution, the Massachusetts constitution of 1780 did not provide for the complete separation of church and state but continued the "Standing Order," the special relationship between church and state established in Puritan times. Under the Standing Order arrangements, local towns and parishes supported public worship in the dominant Congregational churches by taxation. Exceptions were granted, however, for recognized minority groups, such as Baptists, who could use the religious tax assessments of their members to support their own church. In addition, the towns were required by the 1780 constitution to elect annually "public teachers of piety, religion and morality." Apparently, the theory was that the minister provided a civic function as a public teacher of morality, as well as an ecclesiastic function as a minister of the church.[3]

Since the election of the public teacher of morality was by all voters, not just church members, voters in some localities ignored the wishes of the older (and usually Trinitarian) church members and elected Unitarian ministers/teachers of morality. The question then arose as to which group had title to the church property—the majority of the townspeople who had elected the teacher of morality or the majority of members formally affiliated with the church. After a series of lawsuits, the Massachusetts Supreme Court ruled in the Dedham decision of 1820 that church property belonged to the town, rather than to the membership of the local church. After the Dedham decision, more than one hundred parishes decided to become Unitarian, Those in their congregations who remained orthodox Trinitarians withdrew and formed their own new churches. In other cases, the Congregationalists kept the building and the Unitarians built a new meeting house. The result can be seen in many New England towns, where there are two churches around the town common, one Congregational and one Unitarian. Even such church property as communion silver often stayed with the Unitarians (who soon stopped celebrating communion) rather than being moved with the Trinitarians (who continued to celebrate the Eucharist) to their new structure.

In addition to the Unitarian churches arising out of the Congregational controversy, some other traditional churches adopted Unitarianism. Among these was the First Episcopal Church in Boston, King's Chapel, which followed the lead of a new minister, James Freeman, in 1782 in replacing its Trinitarian liturgy with Unitarian phrases. Since this was well before Priestley came to America, Freeman was the first Unitarian minister of the first Unitarian church in the United States.[4]

After the Dedham decision and the split with the Congregationalists, the Unitarians formed the majority church in many New England communities. The Universalists were distinctly different; from their beginnings, they were a minority religion.

The founder of American Universalism, John Murray, was a disciple of the English Universalist preacher James Relly. The Universalists believed that at the Last Judgement, all men would be saved. This doctrine of universal salvation had been considered a heresy in England until 1562.[5]

When Murray left England, he intended to retire in America but soon found himself preaching, first in New Jersey and later up and down the Atlantic coast. He finally settled in Gloucester, Massachusetts in 1779. He organized a group of followers as an independent church and constructed a building for their worship services. The Universalists then applied for exemption from the taxes paid to the parish church, which was, of course, Congregational. The parish refused to grant the exemption on the basis that the Universalists were not a recognized denomination like the Baptists, and the members who had left the Congregational church to join the Universalists had not given any reason to the parish. Further, Murray had not been ordained as a minister in Massachusetts and the church's doctrine of universal salvation undercut the basis of morality—the possibility of punishment at the Last Judgement. The Universalists finally settled the matter by securing incorporation from the legislature and re-ordaining Murray. [6]

In spite of other doctrinal lapses, the Universalists were originally Trinitarian in their beliefs. Eventually in the nineteenth century, a young minister, Hosea Ballou, moved the denomination to the Unitarian position, while still keeping the Universalist name and other beliefs. The Universalist Church of

ATHEISTS, AGNOSTICS, AND DEISTS IN AMERICA

America was formally established in 1833, with Tufts College in Medford, Massachusetts, providing a divinity school for training Universalist ministers..

Apart from omitting reference to the Trinity from their services, the New England Unitarians in the first half of the nineteenth century were little different from the Congregational churches from which they had split. Most still celebrated communion and sang the same Congregational hymns such as "Come Thou Almighty King." (As late as 1953, the Unitarian hymnal contained "Onward Christian Soldiers.") It was over the issue of refusing to celebrate communion that Emerson was forced to resign from the pulpit of the Second Unitarian Church of Boston in 1834. Although he continued to preach at Unitarian churches in the Boston area, he never again held a full-time ministerial post.[7] Theodore Parker, like Emerson a Unitarian minister in the transcendentalist movement, was also asked by the local Unitarian minister's association to resign his post because of his deistic and pantheistic views, but he refused. Like Emerson, Parker continued to preach, but his fellow Unitarian ministers declined to exchange pulpits with him.[8]

Parker shocked many in his denomination when he spoke on "The Transient and Permanent in Christianity" at the ordination of Charles C. Shackford at Hawes Place Church in South Boston. In it he classified as transient all of the Bible, both Old Testament and New, Christian rites and doctrines, and even the personality of Jesus. The permanent aspects of religion are the "great truths which spring up spontaneously in the holy heart." He also said, "If it could be proved that Jesus never lived, still Christianity would stand firm and fear no evil," based on the moral teachings of Christ. Although Parker was not an atheist, as some of his critics claimed, he certainly was not a conventional Unitarian or Christian.[9]

At this point in their history, though, few Unitarians followed Parker and Emerson into transcendentalism. The leading Unitarian in the period before the Civil War was William

UNITARIANS AND UNIVERSALISTS

Ellery Channing, a was minister of Boston's Federal Street Church. While acknowledging that some Biblical writing was metaphorical, Channing continued to believe that many of the miracles reported in the Bible were historical facts, based on the sincerity and passion of those who reported them.[10] He thus remained in the mainstream of Unitarianism, which was not sympathetic to either Jefferson's deism or Emerson's and Parker's transcendentalism. In fact, in 1853 the Executive Committee of the American Unitarian Association issued a creed stating that Unitarians endorsed "belief in the Divine Origin, the Divine Authority and the Divine sanctions of the religion of Jesus Christ."[11]

In the period before the Civil War, there were several efforts to extend Unitarianism beyond New England. During the 1830s, James Freeman Clarke, a friend of Margaret Fuller, established a Unitarian church in Louisville, Kentucky. Clarke went on to serve on the executive committee of the American Unitarian Association and became its secretary in 1859.[12] (Clarke also suggested to Julia Ward Howe that she write "The Battle Hymn of the Republic." [13]) In New York State, there was a church in Buffalo to which President Millard Fillmore and his wife belonged. In 1860 Thomas Starr King, a Universalist minister who had converted to Unitarianism, left Boston to found a Unitarian congregation in San Francisco.

Following the Civil War, Henry W. Bellows, the minister of All Souls Church in New York City, recognized the need for a firmer organizational structure for the Unitarian churches. (Bellows had been the organizer during the Civil War of the United States Sanitary Commission, which was responsible for the care of sick and wounded Union soldiers and their dependent families.) A Unitarian convention was held in 1865 in New York, with almost two hundred churches represented by four hundred delegates. The conference adopted the name of The National Conference of Unitarian Churches and a constitution with a preamble which pledged the members to "the service of God and the building up of the Kingdom of his Son."[14] Some Unitarians felt that the national organization was too conservative and withdrew to form the Free Religious Association in 1867.

The dissidents were in large part followers of Theodore Parker. As we have noted above, Parker repudiated the idea of any external religious authority, including the Bible, and was convinced that true religious faith had to originate in the human spirit. The first convention of the Free Religious Association was held in Boston on May 30, 1867. Among the founders were Ralph Waldo Emerson, Robert Dale Owen, and Lucretia Mott, the suffragist. (Parker had died in 1860.) The organization adopted a constitution which stated that the aims of the association were to promote "the interests of pure religion" and to encourage the "scientific study of theology." All the members were firm believers in evolution. They were strongly anti-Christian and substituted a faith in human nature for a faith in Christ.[15] Although they did not completely reject the Bible, they condemned its use by ministers and priests as a divinely inspired work. They also rejected the use of Sunday as a holy day and campaigned for its secularization as a part of the separation of church and state.[16]

Not all the Unitarians who joined the Free Religious Association severed their ties with Unitarianism. One who did not was John Weiss, the grandson of a German Jew, who was pastor of Unitarian churches in Watertown and New Bedford, Massachusetts. Weiss continued as minister of his churches and as a director of the American Unitarian Association. He called his beliefs "theistic naturalism," which seemed too close to deism for his parishioners, and he eventually stopped preaching.[17] In the years following the establishment of the Free Religious Association in Boston, local societies of people with similar views were established in other cities, generally in the Northeast. They had no formal affiliation with the parent group, however, which disapproved of subsidiary chapters.[18] This lack of organization eventually killed the group.

In addition to facing defections of religious liberals to the

UNITARIANS AND UNIVERSALISTS

Free Religious Association, the Unitarians faced dissension within the organization. Liberal Unitarians in the western part of the United States, who in 1852 had formed the Western Unitarian Conference, remained within the denomination but refused to follow the Eastern establishment's theological views. An 1886 pamphlet issued at the annual meeting of the Western Unitarian Conference stated:

> Within a dozen years or so, seemingly as the result of the breaking over the West of the free religious wave of the East , there has been a movement here, at first quite unnoticed in itself, but becoming more definite in its purpose and more pronounced as it went on, to create a new and different order of Unitarianism in the West. From the beginning, this new Unitarianism has shown an especially warm sympathy with the Free Religions movement, and later, with the Ethical movement; has steadily sought to differentiate itself from the Unitarianism of the East as being "broader" and "more advanced" than that, has long been averse to the use of the Christian name, and for a few years past has been more and more distinctly moving off from even a theistic basis, until now it declares openly and strongly that even belief in God must no longer be declared an essential of Unitarianism.
>
> To avoid misunderstanding, it must be said at the outset, however, that most of the men who are thus endeavoring to remove the Unitarianism of the West onto this new basis, are themselves, personally, believers in God, prayer, and immortality, as they are unquestionably sincere in their expressed wish that all individual Unitarians must be believers in the same. But, they say, all this must be left solely to the individual.... Unitarianism must stand for ethical beliefs and beliefs in certain so-called "principles," but not for belief in anything that will commit it to theism or Christianity...

> The issue before the West is not one of creed or no
> creed. Nobody wants a creed....But this cannot justly be
> made to imply that we have not stood or do not stand for
> any doctrinal belief, as a denomination....We have always
> stood...for the great, simple, primal, self-evidencing faiths
> of religion—God, worship, the immortal life, the suprem-
> acy of character, the spiritual leadership of Jesus....By
> hauling down and destroying our theistic and Christian
> flags and running up in their place the ethical only, I am
> convinced we would seal the fate of Unitarianism as a
> religious movement in the West.[19]

The pamphlet clearly indicates that there must have been
in the West a number of Unitarians who were atheists who
wanted "Principles" instead of "Creeds."As the controversy
continued, the Unitarian headquarters in Boston resolved not to
give assistance "to any church or organization which does not rest
emphatically on the Christian basis." By 1894 the Western
Conference moved to reconcile with the national organization and
adopted a statement of "Things Commonly Believed Among Us"
which included the statements "Unitarianism is a religion of love
to God and love to man" and "We believe that to love the Good
and to live the Good is the supreme thing in religion."

For the next twenty years, the Unitarians appeared to
have beaten back attempts to include non-Christian idealists
within the denomination. Shortly before World War I, though,
two Unitarian ministers began preaching religious humanism—the Reverend John H. Dietrich joined the Unitarians in
Spokane, Washington, after the Reformed church had expelled
him for heresy, and the Reverend Curtis W. Reese, a former
Baptist, began preaching the humanist doctrine at the Unitarian
church in Des Moines, Iowa. Reese stated, "Liberalism is building
a religion that would not be shaken even if the thought of God
were outgrown."[20] At a meeting of Unitarian ministers sponsored
by the Harvard Summer School of Theology in July 1920, there

was a movement to oust the humanists from the denomination. The humanists were, however, defended by other liberal ministers, including "evolutionary theists", who declared that evolution was God's method of creation. The outcome was that the absence of a creed for members of the denomination was extended to the ministers.[21]

In 1933, Dietrich (who by then had moved to Minneapolis), Reese, and sixteen other Unitarian ministers signed the "Humanist Manifesto," which included the statement, "We are convinced that the time has passed for theism, deism, modernism, and the several varieties of 'newthought.'"[22] In addition to the Unitarians, fourteen others signed the Manifesto, including the philosopher and educator John Dewey. We shall discuss the Manifesto further in the chapter on Humanism. Although the Manifesto did not have an immediate effect, after World War II humanism fueled the growth of the Unitarian movement.[23] Most of the Unitarian humanists probably are agnostics or atheists.

"Probably" is used in the previous sentence because the Unitarian Universalists do not require their members to subscribe to any particular set of beliefs or even to say what their beliefs are. Nevertheless, three Unitarian Universalist ministers who recently wrote short essays on "Why I Am a Humanist" all reject supernatural forces and the idea of a personal god while endorsing reason and rationality as guides to human actions.[24] It is likely that those in their congregations who classify themselves as humanists hold similar atheistic beliefs.

It should be noted here that the term "religious humanism" is used differently by various groups. Dietrich, the Unitarian Universalist minister, gave this name to his set of atheistic and science-friendly beliefs. On the other hand, a 1997 book, *The New Religious Humanists: A Reader,* includes only authors whose beliefs are explicitly based on the Judeo-Christian tradition. The essays have such titles as "Christian Humanism in a Postmodern Age" and "The Christian Writer in a Fragmented Culture."[25]

ATHEISTS, AGNOSTICS, AND DEISTS IN AMERICA

In the 1950s, discussions began between the Unitarians and Universalists about possible merger of the denominations. As a first step, the two young people's groups, American Unitarian Youth and Universalist Youth Fellowship, merged in 1953. The parent groups then discussed a full merger. Before the final agreement, there was extended discussion over whether the wording of the introductory clause should refer to "our Judeo-Christian heritage," which was finally included in the merger agreement signed in 1960.[26] The Unitarian Universalist Association in the 1990s initiated a media campaign to attract new members, employing both newspaper advertisements and radio announcements. It currently has a sophisticated website on the Internet at www.uua.org. The site is headed with the motto "Affirming the Inherent Worth and Dignity of Every Person" and contains links to congregations, programs and services, and the UU magazine *World.*

As the twentieth century draws to a close, the Unitarian Universalists continue to discuss the differences between those UUs who are humanist in orientation and those favoring a faith-based religious commitment. At a convocation of Unitarian ministers in Hot Springs, Arkansas, in 1995, the ministers were unable to agree on adding the phrase "a critical trust in the power of reason" to a proposed affirmation "that the heart of our faith is a sense of the holy." In an informal poll at the 1997 General Assembly of the Unitarian Universalist Association, half or more of the delegates identified themselves as humanists.[27] In a subsequent survey on theological perspectives of UU members distributed in 108,000 copies of the September/October 1997 issue of the denominational magazine *World,* as well as on the UU website, 46.1 percent of approximately 9,000 responders identified themselves as "humanist."[28] In the individual congregations, though, the proportion of humanists varies. In a 1998 letter to the editor of the magazine *World,* a member of the Spokane, Washington, Unitarian Universalist church reports that in his congregation the "New Age/spiritualism group" now constitutes a majority. The humanists now meet separately in the church building once a month, with many also attending the regular services.[29] The location of Spokane is significant, since this is the church at which Dietrich first preached on Unitarian humanism. There also was a 1998 letter in *The Humanist,* the journal of The American Humanist Association, from the president of a UU congregation in Pennsylvania stating that she was leaving the UU's and joining the humanists because of the marginalization of humanists in her church.[30]

According to an article in *The Humanist,* the largest single organization of humanists in the United States is the Unitarian Universalist Association.[31] Therefore, the future of organized atheism in this country will depend in part on the outcome of the discussions now going on within the UU churches and in the national Unitarian Universalist Association about the place of humanism in their organizations..

In the next chapter we shall discuss the Ethical Culture movement, which in some significant ways is similar to the Unitarian Universalists.

CHAPTER IX

THE ETHICAL CULTURE MOVEMENT

In many ways, the Ethical Culture movement is similar to Unitarianism. Both consider themselves to be religious organizations, and both reject any formal creed or set of beliefs required of members. Both are based on local congregations that meet each Sunday and provide Sunday Schools for children of members, As noted in the previous chapter, Unitarianism evolved from the Congregationalists, a Protestant Christian denomination in New England, and its early members were former Congregationalists. The Ethical Culture movement, on the other hand, was founded by Felix Adler, a former Jew, and many of its early members were Jewish.

Adler was born in 1851 in the town of Alzei in the Rhineland section of Germany. When Felix was six years old, his family emigrated to New York City, where his father became rabbi of Temple Emanu-El, one of the leading Jewish Reform congregations in the country. In New York, Felix attended Columbia grammar school and graduated in 1870 with high honors from Columbia College. He then returned to Germany for graduate work at the Universities of Berlin and Heidelberg, where he studied Semitics (the language, literature, and history of Semitic peoples} in preparation for becoming a rabbi.[1]

While in Germany, Adler was exposed to the writings of Immanuel Kant. Two of Kant's ideas proved particularly influential—that the existence or nonexistence of God could not be demonstrated by "pure reason" and that morality could be established without any reference to theology.[2]

Adler received his Ph.D., *summa cum laude,* from Heidelberg in 1873 and returned to New York City, where he was invited to give a sermon at his father's temple. His sermon expressed his liberal feelings on religion, and afterward some members asked if he believed in God. He replied that he did, "but not in your God."[3] Adler soon made the final break with Judaism and accepted an appointment as professor of Oriental languages and literature at Cornell University in Ithaca, New York. Although he was a popular teacher, he was attacked as an atheist and resigned his professorship in 1876 to return to New York City.[4]

In New York Adler met with others who shared his feeling that religion should emphasize ethical rather than theological questions. On May 15, 1876, he and his friends founded the Society for Ethical Culture as "a religious society which shall be practical as well as spiritual, and unhampered by sectarian religious dogmas." Adler was employed as "Lecturer." There was a fifteen-man Board of Trustees, of which Adler was an ex-officio member. In practice, Adler ran the organization.[5]

Two years later *The New York Times* reported

> The Society for Ethical Culture, which has attracted much attention and excited considerable interest of late in this community, is not quite two years old. It will be 24 months this coming May....A number of men of different nationalities, including German, Frenchmen, Italians, Englishmen, and Americans founded it, having felt, as they say, the need in the city of a permanent and effective organization to support the cause of enlightenment. [6]

In addition to heading the Society for Ethical Culture, Adler was an active member of the Free Religious Association mentioned in the previous chapter. At the time he joined the FRA in 1875, members included Emerson, Lucretia Mott, Wendell Philllips, and Julia Ward Howe. Adler had in his youth read Emerson and was especially impressed with Emerson's thoughts on free religion and self-reliance.[7] In 1878 Adler was elected to the presidency of the Free Religious Association. As president, he felt that although the association had served as a useful forum for religious liberals, it was short on programs for action. He proposed that the association endow chairs of the science of religion in leading universities and establish local chapters to promote free religion. At the annual meeting of the Association in 1882, Adler asked

> What has Boston done for the honor of our principles? What

great charitable movement has found its source here among those who maintain the principle of freedom in religion? What living thing for the good of mankind, for the perfecting of morality among yourselves and others emanated within the last twenty years from the Free Religious circles of this city? I say to you, friends, these annual meetings will not answer.[8]

Because of its lack of a social-action program, Adler resigned the presidency of the Free Religious Association in 1882. In the meantime, he had made sure that his Society for Ethical Culture emphasized "deed not creed." In 1877, a year after its founding, the society added a District Nursing Department, a forerunner of today's Visiting Nurse Service. The following year, 1878, the society started a free kindergarten for poor children, the first in New York, and a Workingman's School, specializing in vocational education. In 1882 Adler was appointed to the New York State Tenement House Commission. He also became active in politics and supported Henry George, the single-tax advocate, in his campaign for Mayor of New York City.[9]

Because in some ways the society acted like a church, it soon had to perform certain rites for members. In addition to providing funerals, it organized a company in 1885 to own and operate the Mt. Pleasant Cemetery in Hawthorne, New York, which still exists. The society also persuaded the New York State legislature to pass in 1888 a bill authorizing the leader of the New York society to solemnize marriages in the same way as would a minister or priest.[10]

During the last quarter of the nineteenth century, ethical societies were founded in a number of other cities, starting with Chicago in 1882 and followed by Philadelphia in 1885 and St. Louis in 1886. The Chicago society resulted from a series of lectures Adler gave in that city which attracted a number of men of influence and wealth. To lead it, Adler provided one of his young New York apprentices, William Salter.

Salter was the son of a devout Congregational family in Iowa. He graduated from Knox College in Illinois in 1871 and entered the Yale Divinity School. He discovered, however, that orthodox Christianity was not in accordance with his evolving beliefs and transferred to the Harvard Divinity School in 1873, intending to become a Unitarian minister. After his graduation in 1876, a combination of ill health and religious doubts caused him to become a sheep herder for two years. Then in 1879 he met Adler and joined him in New York two years later.

Salter's first years as leader of the Chicago society were successful, but his position on the guilt of the anarchists arrested for the bomb throwing in Haymarket Square in 1886 was highly controversial. Along with a Unitarian minister, Salter organized a petition drive to ask the governor for clemency for the eight convicted anarchists. Many Chicagoans, including members of his congregation, felt that support for the anarchists was equivalent to treason, and attendance at the meetings dropped drastically. In 1892, Salter transferred to the Philadelphia Ethical Culture Society, which had been founded six years previously.[11]

The New York Society for Ethical Culture, however, remained paramount. From its founding until 1910, it held weekly meetings in rented halls, first in Chickering Hall and later in Carnegie Hall. In 1904 the Ethical Culture School moved into new headquarters on Central Park West at 63rd Street, and three years later the meeting house was built adjoining the school.[12] Adler continued to be the most important figure in the society until his death in 1933.

Among younger men in the society, perhaps the most influential was John Lovejoy Elliott, who was born in 1868 on a farm in Princeton, Illinois, and attended a one-room schoolhouse. His was not, though, an ordinary farm family. His mother, Elizabeth, was a step-daughter of Owen Lovejoy, an abolitionist and friend of Abraham Lincoln. Elliott chose to go to Cornell University, where he was popular and was elected president of his senior class. While at Cornell, he heard a lecture by Adler which changed his life. They corresponded, and after graduation Elliott went off to the University of Halle in Germany, where he wrote his doctoral thesis on "Prisons as Reformatories." Elliot returned to New York City in 1894 to work as an assistant to Adler at a salary of $700 per year. He was active both in the society headquarters and in the organizations associated with the society known as the Hudson Guild, which included a gymnasium, library, and employment bureau.[13]

Upon Adler's death, Elliott was elected senior leader, and he attempted to broaden the membership base beyond the upper-class group who had been attracted to Adler. He organized a worker's fellowship, which was granted recognition on the society's council. The council did succeed in bringing in new members. It was, however, suspected of being infiltrated by Communists and led to loss of membership in the parent organization until the council was dissolved in the early fifties. Another innovation introduced by Elliott was the broadcast of Sunday meetings of the New York society over radio station WQXR, which have continued for many years and were still being aired in 1998.[14]

Among recent leaders of the Ethical Culture movement is Edward L. Ericson. Born in a small southern town, he was brought up as a conservative Christian. Like several other Ethical Culture leaders, he lost his faith during adolescence and eventually found the Unitarians. After attending divinity school, he served as a humanist minister of a Unitarian congregation. Then in 1959 he became leader of the ethical society in Washington, D.C. His service in Washington was followed by a stint as senior leader in Felix Adler's ethical society in New York City. He also served a term as president of the national federation, the American Ethical Union.[15] In 1988, Ericson wrote a book, *The Humanist Way*, which is an excellent introduction to religious humanism.

At the time of Adler's death in 1933, the American Ethical Union reported 3,300 members in seven societies.[16] These seven societies were all in urban centers. Following World War II, many of the members in these cities moved to the suburbs, and accordingly a number of new chapters of the American Ethical Union were formed. In the New York area, there are now eleven societies in the boroughs of New York City, Westchester County, Long Island, and New Jersey, where once there was only one. There were also new societies formed in the South and on the West Coast. By the end of the twentieth century, there were twenty-five societies in thirteen states and the District of Columbia.[17] Total membership in 1998 was approximately 3,000, little changed from the 1930's.[18] The society's greater geographical diversity, however, probably gives it a better chance of surviving in the twenty-first century.

CHAPTER X

THE AMERICAN HUMANIST ASSOCIATION

It is appropriate to introduce this review of the American Humanist Association with a statement by the Association's philosopher, Corliss Lamont, in the first chapter of his book *The Philosophy of Humanism*:

> Since the earliest days of philosophic reflection in ancient times in both the East and West, thinkers of depth and acumen have advanced the simple proposition that the chief end of human life is to work for the happiness of humans upon this earth and within the confines of the Nature that is our home. This philosophy of enjoying, developing, and making available to everyone the abundant material, cultural, and spiritual goods of this natural world is profound in its implications, yet easy to understand and congenial to common sense. This human-centered theory of life has remained relatively unheeded during long periods of history. While it has gone under a variety of names, it is a philosophy that I believe is most accurately designated as *Humanism*.[1]

The term "humanist" was first used during the Renaissance to describe those scholars whose interests were in the Greek and Roman classics, which they thought were the best education for man and would allow him to shape his own life. Humanists valued pleasure rather than medieval asceticism and looked to the philosophy of Epicurus as a guide. In the fifteenth century, Erasmus and Thomas More were considered humanists.

Humanism is used in this book, however, in Lamont's sense of a philosophy that recognizes human beings as part of nature and rejects the supernatural beliefs of conventional religions in favor of values based on human experience and culture. To distinguish this use of the word from the humanism of Erasmus and his contemporary Christian followers, the qualifier "naturalistic humanism" is now often used by members of the American Humanist Association.

On the other hand, most Unitarian Universalists and members of Ethical Culture societies prefer to refer to their beliefs as "religious humanism" on the basis that their ethical and spiritual beliefs, while nontheistic, are essentially religious in nature. In a 1961 Supreme Court case, the Court held that the Constitution extended the full protection of the freedom of religion clause to a nontheistic humanist who was a member of the Washington, D.C., Ethical Society. Unfortunately, in a footnote to the opinion, Justice Hugo Black referred to the humanist religion as "Secular Humanism." This has become a pejorative term used by the religious right to criticize all non-theists. As noted above, most practicing humanists prefer the terms "religious humanism" or "naturalistic humanism."[2]

In the chapter on Unitarian Universalists, we noted that in 1933 a group of Unitarian ministers joined other like-minded individuals to produce A Humanist Manifesto. Actually, the genesis of this Manifesto was a little magazine called The New Humanist which was published by students at the University of Chicago commencing in 1927. The students also formed a Humanist Fellowship to promote "building a society in which every human being shall have the greatest possible opportunity for the best possible life."[3] Many of those active in the Humanist Fellowship were students of Dr. A. Eustis Haydon, a professor of comparative religions at the University of Chicago and part-time Unitarian minister at the Unitarian church in Madison, Wisconsin.

During these years, there was considerable movement of people between the Unitarians, ethical culturists, and humanists.

THE AMERICAN HUMANIST ASSOCIATION

As noted in the chapter on Unitarians and Universalists, the majority of the signers of the 1933 *Humanist Manifesto* were Unitarian ministers. Commencing in 1930, the managing editor of *The New Humanist* was Edwin H. Wilson, former minister of the First Unitarian Church in Dayton, Ohio. Another editor, Harold Buschman, left the magazine in 1934 to work in the Ethical Culture office in New York City. Raymond B. Bragg, who replaced Buschman as associate editor of *The New Humanist,* was also secretary of the Western Unitarian Conference, whose headquarters were in Chicago. Bragg was a student at the Unitarian Meadville Seminary at the time it moved from Pennsylvania to Chicago, where he was exposed to the humanist ideas of Dr. Haydon, Curtis Reese, and others. Bragg then became a Unitarian minister in Evanston, Illinois, for two years before assuming the executive position with the Western Unitarian Conference.[4].

It was Bragg who initiated the discussions that led to the *Humanist Manifesto*. In his travels for the Unitarians, he talked to a number of sympathizers with the humanist movement. Back in Chicago discussions continued, and it was decided to ask a lecturer at the university, Roy Wood Sellars, to write a first draft based on ideas furnished by Bragg, which Sellars did. This draft document was extensively edited and revised by a committee of Wilson, Bragg, Haydon, and Reese, and the final document was sent out for comment to a limited number of people on April 1, 1933.[5]

Both the draft of *The Humanist Manifesto* and the final document contain fifteen theses. Of these, the third, sixth, and fourteenth proved to be the most controversial. The third thesis rejected the dualism of mind and body and thus implicitly the concept of a soul. The sixth rejected theism, deism, and other theologies involving a supernatural God. The document was not confined to philosophical and religious concepts. The fourteenth thesis called for a "socialized and cooperative economic order" to make possible a more equitable distribution of the world's goods.[6]

ATHEISTS, AGNOSTICS, AND DEISTS IN AMERICA

Some of those to whom the draft was sent, including the philosopher and educator John Dewey, signed the document with no suggested changes. Others, including some humanists, felt so strongly about the sixth article rejecting theism and deism that they refused to sign. Four of the humanist Unitarian ministers to whom the draft was sent declined to sign because they feared the Manifesto amounted to a "creed." W. Frank Smith, a director of the Boston Ethical Society, and V.T. Thayer, the Educational Director of Ethical Culture Schools, signed the Manifesto,[7] but the leaders of the national American Ethical Union felt the thrust was too secular and refused to sign it.[8] In an article in their publication, the *Standard*, they also echoed the Unitarian objection that the Manifesto amounted to a creed.

The publication of the Manifesto received wide publicity. *Time* magazine in its May 15, 1933, issue gave a generally favorable review, concluding, "Humanism in the United States is very much alive." On the other hand, many newspapers such as the Bristol, Connecticut *Press,* were strongly critical. Although *The New York Times* did not cover the story, the *New York Herald Tribune,* the *Chicago Tribune*, and the *Boston Evening Transcript* did. [9]

Because many of the signers of the Manifesto had reservations about some of its statements, there soon were calls to revise the document. These were brought to a head in 1939 by Dr. Charles Francis Potter, one of the signatories and author of the 1933 book *Humanizing Religion*. Potter wrote letters to most of the original signatories suggesting that the document be revised and published again. This was referred to a committee of the Humanist Press Association, but the committee never met, and the idea was dropped.[10]

In 1941 Edwin Wilson, the editor of *The New Humanist,* moved to Schenectady, New York, where he became minister of the Unitarian church there. The name of the magazine's sponsor was changed from the Humanist Press Association to the American Humanist Association, and the magazine itself dropped the "new" from its title to become *The Humanist*. In addition to his duties as editor of the magazine, Wilson became executive director of the AHA.[11]

In 1952 the American Humanist Association along with the American Ethical Union became founding members of the International Humanist and Ethical Union, headquartered in Utrecht, the Netherlands. In 1967 the two organizations met jointly in Philadelphia to explore areas of common ground, and the following year jointly set up the Council on Humanist and Ethical Concerns to represent the humanist/ethical point of view in Washington, D.C.[12] They also collaborated in jointly sponsoring the publication of *The Humanist* during Paul Kurtz's period as editor of the magazine. In 1978, the AEU withdrew as co-publisher and a new editor was elected.[13] It appears that the relationship between the two organizations depended heavily on the presence of Kurtz, and the groups fell apart when Kurtz was no longer *The Humanist*'s editor.

In 1953, the twentieth anniversary of the original Manifesto, *The Humanist* published a symposium containing the views of the twenty-seven surviving signers on the question of how well the document had stood the test of time and what changes should be made if a new document were issued. Most of the signers felt that the bulk of the document was still valid, but several suggested changing point fourteen which favored establishing "a socialized and cooperative economic order," which had been interpreted by some critics of humanism as an endorsement of Soviet communism . Instead, it was suggested any new document emphasize the need to voluntarily cooperate in a free society to achieve a more equitable distribution of goods. In the end, it took another twenty years before a new Manifesto was issued.

The impetus for a new manifesto came from Edwin Wilson, the first editor of *The Humanist,* who suggested that Paul Kurtz undertake to draft and circulate the new document in time to issue it in 1973, the fortieth anniversary of what was now called *Humanist Manifesto I.* Although the various suggested changes to the original draft were difficult to reconcile, Kurtz persevered, and the final document received an overwhelmingly favorable response from well-known leaders. Among the signers were Andrei Sakharov, the leading Soviet dissident, Gunnar Myrdal, Swedish scientist and Nobel Prize winner, Sir Julian Huxley, first president of UNESCO (United Nations Educational Scientific and Cultural Organization), as well as Betty Friedan, founder of NOW (National Organization for Women), Alan Guttmacher, president of Planned Parenthood, civil rights leaders James Farmer and A. Philip Randolph, poet John Ciardi, and author Isaac Azimov.

Humanist Manifesto II was much longer than *Humanist Manifesto I.* Like the first document, the new Manifesto was organized by theses, now grown from fifteen to seventeen.

These seventeen were grouped in five categories:

1. The RELIGION section rejects belief in the supernatural in favor of testing any account of nature against scientific evidence and denies any divine purpose for the human species. It affirms that humans are the product of evolutionary forces and denies that life survives the death of the body.

2. The ETHICS section states that moral values derive their value from human experience, rather than from theology or ideology. It suggests that the scientific method be extended to the solution of human problems while maintaining compassion and empathy.

3. The section on THE INDIVIDUAL proclaims the dignity of the individual as a central humanist value. It endorses maximum individual autonomy consonant with social responsibility. It endorses the right to birth control, abortion, and divorce, as well as freedom of any kind of sexual conduct that does not harm others.

4. The DEMOCRATIC SOCIETY section strongly endorses the usual civil liberties and deplores increased invasion of privacy. It urges extension of participatory democracy and continued separation of church and state. While no longer recommending the "socialized and cooperative" economic order of the first

Manifesto, it leaves the door open for alternatives to capitalism. It proposes a minimum guaranteed annual income and universal education.

5. The WORLD COMMUNITY section states that war is obsolete and calls for worldwide ecological planning and elimination of extreme differences in wealth and income on a worldwide basis.[14]

Of course, the above is an incomplete summary of four tightly packed pages, but it should give the flavor of the document, which has less emphasis on religion and more on individual freedom than its predecessor. *Humanist Manifesto II* received even more publicity than its predecessor, including a page one article in *The New York Times* on August 26, 1973. It was extensively discussed in editorial comments and articles for a number of months. Many of the commentators were favorable to the document, but the religious conservatives were irate. The *National Review* said the signers included "the greatest concentration of eccentric intelligence since Bertrand Russell dined alone." The document has repeatedly been cited by the religious right as part of an alleged international humanist conspiracy.[15]

In 1987, a group of Quaker humanists became a chartered chapter of the AHA as the Humanist Society of Friends. This consolidated several breakaway groups of Quakers in Yellow Springs, Ohio, and Los Angeles who were dissatisfied with the implied theism in the traditional Quaker meetings. Since 1990 the chapter has been an incorporated division of AHA, responsible for its religious humanist programs.[16] Through its Division of Humanist Certification, AHA members for one or more years may apply for a certificate which entitles them to the same legal rights as ministers and rabbis to officiate at weddings and other ceremonies, including same-sex unions.[17]

The American Humanist Association is currently considering a *Humanist Manifesto III*. On the silver anniversary of the second Manifesto, a symposium was held, with remarks by Paul Kurtz and eleven of the original signers published in the September/October 1998 issue of *The Humanist*. Most of those commenting agreed that the major changes in the world in the past quarter century, such as the dissolution of the Soviet Union, the increased use of computers, and the genetic revolution warrant the consideration of a new document.[18]

At the end of the twentieth century, the American Humanist Association appears to be prospering. Their organizational format differs from both the Unitarian Universalists and the Ethical Cultural societies in that the humanists function through local chapters, which may meet monthly or only occasionally, rather than having weekly meetings on Sunday in imitation of the churches, as the other two organizations do. The American Humanist Association has seventy-three chapters in thirty states and the District of Columbia.[19] The total membership of the association is about 5,000 and has been steadily increasing. Circulation of *The Humanist* in 1998 was 7,500, compared with 118,000 for the Unitarian Universalist publication, *World*.[20] The Humanists have started a fund-raising campaign for a national headquarters in Washington, D.C., which has already raised over $100,000.

As is the case for the Unitarian Universalists and the Ethical Culturists, the Humanists have their own website on the Internet at www.humanist.net. It is a sophisticated site with links to the local chapters, many of which have their own websites and/or e-mail addresses. There also are links to such documents as *Humanist Manifesto I* and *Humanist Manifesto II*.

Finally, since we started this chapter with a quotation from Corliss Lamont, we shall close it with a note about him. Lamont was the son of a partner in J.P. Morgan. Born in 1902, he graduated from Harvard University in 1924, *magna cum laude*, followed by graduate work at Oxford and Columbia universities, where he received his Ph.D. in 1932. Lamont taught at Columbia, Cornell, and Harvard universities and was the author of sixteen books. He was a director of the American Civil Liberties Union from 1932 to 1954 and won famous court decisions over Senator Joseph McCarthy and the CIA. At his death in 1995 he bequeathed his mansion and estate in Ossining, New York, to the American Humanist Association for use as a library. With this new library, a national headquarters in the offing, and an organizational format well suited for further growth, the AHA looks toward a bright future.

CHAPTER XI

AMERICAN ATHEISTS (ORGANIZED AND UNORGANIZED)

In the previous chapters, we have encountered a number of organizations such as the Free Religious Association and the American Ethical Union, the majority of whose members were atheists but who chose not to refer to atheism in their name. In part, this was because their purposes were broader than the promotion of atheism. Probably, they also were influenced by the likelihood that the term "atheist" is still regarded as a pejorative by most Americans.

An exception is the American Atheist Association of Austin, Texas, an organization founded by Madalyn Murray O'Hair in 1963. Madalyn Murray was born in 1919 and grew up in Pittsburgh, Pennsylvania, in a family that was wealthy until the stock market crash of 1929. Madalyn happily attended the Presbyterian Sunday school and church services. Im 1941 she married William Murray, Jr. and followed her husband into the armed forces by joining the Women's Army Corps, where she served as an officer in Africa, Italy, and France. In an autobiographical note in her book *An Atheist Epic,* she claims to have been educated as an engineer, an attorney, a psychiatric social worker, a mathematician, and a cryptographer—and to have practiced in each of these fields. In the same autobiographical note she states, "I have been married twice and have had four love affairs in between."[1]

With her first husband, Bill Murray, she had two children, William Murray III and Jon Garth Murray. Following her divorce from Murray, she married her second husband, Richard O'Hair, in 1965. They adopted Bill's daughter, Robin, who became Robin Murray-O'Hair.

AMERICAN ATHEISTS

It is not clear when Madalyn became an atheist, but in a 1989 interview she stated that she began to doubt the truth of the Bible when she was in the fifth or sixth grade.[2] Her atheism came to the fore when her son Bill transferred from a private school to the Baltimore public schools in 1962. During a vacation in France that summer she and Bill, who had decided that he was also an atheist, mutually agreed that he would not participate in the morning prayer that began the day at his public school. She so notified the superintendent of secondary schools in Baltimore. The superintendent was shocked at the request and suggested as a compromise that Bill could remain silent and move his lips. Mother and son rejected the suggestion and decided that Bill would refuse to attend school until he was no longer required to attend the prayer service.[3]

Eventually, Bill was readmitted, but he and his mother were continually harassed. Madalyn filed a complaint with the Baltimore Board of Education about the way her son had been treated as a result of his refusal to join in the prayers at his public school. The case was heard by the Baltimore City Superior Court, the Maryland Court of Appeals, and, eventually the Supreme Court of the United States (*Murray* v. *Curlett*.) The Supreme Court, by an eight to one decision, declared that prayer in the public schools violated the First Amendment of the Constitution.[4] Unfortunately, the ordeal so affected Bill that he left home, became addicted to drugs, and eventually embraced organized religion.[5] He has since written a vitriolic book about his experiences with his mother.[6]

The case was widely publicized and Madalyn acquired a national reputation. She used the opportunity to found the American Atheist Association in the same year. She moved to Austin, Texas, where she established the organization's headquarters and edited the *American Atheist* magazine.

During the 1980s, the American Atheist Association prospered. According to *The New York Times*, Madalyn's television program *American Atheist Forum* was carried by 140 cable

133

systems and her mailing list reached 50,000. The organization, however, ran into problems in the 1990s. At that time, Madalyn's younger son by her first marriage, Jon Murray, was president of the organization and Robin Murray-O'Hair, the daughter of her estranged son, Bill, was editor of the organization's magazine. The Internal Revenue Service claimed that the two of them and Madalyn owed $1.5 million in back taxes for having used the organization's money for personal purposes. The claim was settled in 1996 for $29,210 from Jon Murray and $7,577 from Robin, while the claim against Madalyn was dismissed.[7]

Then in September of 1996, the three disappeared, leaving behind their Austin home as well as three pet Scotch terriers, two cars, and their personal bank accounts. Moreover, $600,000 of the organization's money was missing.[8] In March 1999 *The New York Times* reported that David R. Waters, who had previously been convicted for theft from the organization, had been arrested as a possible suspect in the murder of the Murray family.[9]

Ellen Johnson, a New Jersey housewife, succeeded Jon Murray as the American Atheists Association's president. She told *The New York Times* in late 1997 that the group's current membership was about 2,500.[10] In spite of the problems, though, the organization has an impressive website, continues to have a cable-access TV show in fifty markets, and continues to publish *The American Atheist* magazine. Obviously, within its small membership base the America Atheists Association continues to have some generous contributors.

In addition to the American Atheist Association, mention should be made of the Freedom from Religion Foundation, a nonprofit group headquartered in Madison, Wisconsin. Founded in 1978, the foundation claims 3,500 members. Like the American Atheist Association, the Freedom Foundation has chapters throughout the country, including one in the unlikely location of Talladega, Alabama, in the heart of the Bible Belt. In the Freedom Hall of the Talladega chapter are quotations from Jefferson, Paine, and Darrow, as well as a bust of Robert Ingersoll. The membership of fifty in the local chapter is apparently stable.[11]

Of course, the organized atheists represent a tiny percentage of the more than 1.5 million atheists listed for North America in the *1999 Statistical Abstracts of the United States*. By nature, most atheists are not joiners but are content to have found their own set of beliefs (or non-beliefs), without any urge to convince others. The generally negative attitude of the majority of Americans toward atheism further discourages their public identification.

On the other hand, the development of the Internet and the World Wide Web has allowed atheists to communicate and express their views without identifying themselves or paying dues to a national organization. Because the web is so changeable, we will not attempt to list atheist websites here, but as of the fall of 1999 there were a number of sites that provided links to other atheist sites around the globe, including lists of atheist sites by city and town for each state of the Union, organized for ease of search.

This chapter concludes the historical section of the book. The next chapter will be devoted to an analysis of why the growth of atheism, agnosticism, and deism in America has been so slow.

CHAPTER XII

THE SLOW GROWTH OF AMERICAN DEISM AND ATHEISM

As we have seen in Chapter III, many of the Founding Fathers were deists. Thomas Jefferson, a deist and a Unitarian, wrote," I confidently expect that the present generation will see Unitarianism become the general religion of the United States."[1] Of course, he was mistaken in this forecast, and Unitarianism, along with deism, agnosticism, and atheism, has been embraced by less than two million people, a small minority of the American population.

In Europe, on the other hand, there were in 1998 more than 23 million people who classified themselves as atheists.[2] Since there were few atheists in Europe before the eighteenth century, this growth of atheism in Europe was contemporaneous with the lack of growth in America.

There is no single reason for the slowness of growth of nonbelievers in the United States. Further, this characteristic lack of growth persisted throughout the period from the early nineteenth century to the dawn of the twenty-first. Throughout this volume, we have identified individual atheists, agnostics, and deists who could have assumed leadership positions in a movement away from traditional religions. However, none of them did so. Robert Owen, Fanny Wright, and the communitarians were more interested in propagating their theories of socialism and in abolition of slavery than in convincing others to adopt their deistic views, and in any case their communitarian movement died with them. The same can be said of Emerson, Thoreau, and the transcendentalists. Emerson's belief that Nature, rather than the Bible, was the best source of truth, was shared by a small group of followers, but not by most members of the Unitarian

THE SLOW GROWTH OF AMERICAN DEISM AND ATHEISM

church to which he belonged. Transcendentalism, like communitarianism, never attracted enough support to survive its founders. In the latter half of the nineteenth century, Robert Ingersoll was recognized as a powerful spokesman for agnosticism, but he made no attempt to organize his followers. Nor did Clarence Darrow, also a magnetic speaker, create a church of his disciples.

Yet, during the same period, the Church of Jesus Christ of Latter-Day Saints, popularly known as Mormons, grew from the vision of one man, Joseph Smith, to an organization with four million members in the United States and an estimated nine million members worldwide. Their success has involved more than acceptance of their beliefs, which many outsiders find strange. More important was their formation of supportive communities and encouragement of their young people to marry within the faith.[3] The Mormons have also carried out a worldwide proselytizing effort requiring young Mormons to serve two years as missionaries for their church.

Apart from successful organization and active recruitment, it seems possible that in America the theistic religions have grown much more rapidly than the atheistic or agnostic groups because many people derive deep satisfaction from their belief in God. This supposition was born out by a recent study by Michael Schermer and Frank Sulloway, an M.I.T. scientist, who conducted a poll to determine why people believed in God and why they thought others believed in God. Although the leading reason given for a personal belief in God was the good design of the universe, the largest response to the question of why others believed was "comfort."[4]

It is difficult, if not impossible, for atheism to offer the comfort that theistic religion offers. A God who answers prayers can be turned to for help in solving problems ranging from illness to marital difficulties. Further, belief in an afterlife offers compensation for a miserable life on earth and the possibility again to see loved ones who have died. Atheism cannot compete with these beliefs in terms of offering comfort.

Of course, this desire in America for the comfort of religion does not explain why the same influence has not similarly affected Europeans, who have embraced atheism to a much greater extent than Americans. Probably most important is the fact that the anti-religious intellectual climate in Europe established by Hume, Voltaire, and Diderot was never duplicated in America. Many of the educated upper class in France were followers of Voltaire and Diderot. Their counterparts in Germany admired Friedrich Nietzsche, who also opposed Christianity. The American upper class in the nineteenth century, in contrast, was composed in large part of self-made tycoons such as Andrew Carnegie and John D. Rockefeller, who carried along to their new social status and positions of influence their traditional Christian views. To the extent that members of the middle class emulated the upper class, the Europeans tended towards atheism and the Americans toward traditional religions.

It may be that our culture is much less impressed by rational arguments than that in Europe. Certainly, one does not see in European papers the astrological horoscopes that are a feature of many U.S. newspapers, including the giant Gannett chain. According to one survey, 63 percent of readers check their daily horoscope in the newspaper.[5] Other Americans believe in UFO's, alien abductees, and communication with the dead through spiritualists. Michael Schermer writes, "The reason people believe in weird things is because they want to. It feels good. It is comforting. It is consoling."[6] Although these "weird" beliefs are held by only a minority of Americans, this minority, at least, would be unlikely to accept rational arguments against the existence of God.

Another possible reason for the difference in acceptance of atheism in Europe and the United States is the differences in the institutions of higher education. In Europe, most of the prestigious universities such as the Sorbonne in France and the

THE SLOW GROWTH OF AMERICAN DEISM AND ATHEISM

Universities of Heidelberg and Berlin in Germany have been supported by the state. In America, particularly in the nineteenth century, the great universities such as Harvard, Yale, and Princeton were private institutions with a strong religious affiliation. At these three, as well as at many of the leading smaller colleges such as Amherst, Bowdoin, and Williams, daily attendance at morning chapel services was compulsory. In 1886 Harvard was the first major American university to do away with compulsory chapel. However, until the middle of the twentieth century, Harvard suspended all morning classes during the period of the religious chapel service to give students the opportunity to attend.[7] Yale University's requirement for chapel attendance by all students was not abolished until 1926.[8] Bowdoin College required chapel attendance until after World War II. The daily religious indoctrination of many of America's future leaders would tend to produce fewer atheists than the religious laissez-faire policy of the European universities.

A further reason for the slow growth of adherents to atheism in the second half of the twentieth century in America is the strong anti-Communist feeling, particularly during the 1950s and 1960s. Although most American Communists, as followers of Karl Marx, have been atheists, they always have been small in number, peaking at about 75,000 members in 1939 and declining to about 2,000 by the end of the century. Nevertheless, the phrase "Godless Communist" stuck in public consciousness and may have deterred some people who otherwise would have explored atheism as an alternative to Christianity from doing so.

For all the above reasons, the growth of atheism in America in the twentieth century was slow. The next chapter will explore whether in the twenty-first century the influence of American scientists, who tend to be rationalistic in their philosophic outlook, might have an effect similar to the influence in Europe of their atheistic and deistic philosophers in the nineteenth and twentieth centuries.

CHAPTER XIII

THE FUTURE OF AMERICAN ATHEISM AND DEISM

As a basis for attempting to forecast the future of atheism and deism in America, we shall briefly analyze how a person comes to his or her religious beliefs. One's religion is probably determined by one or more of the following five factors:

1. The religion of one's parents, reinforced by the Sunday School of the church attended by the parents.

2. The religion of one's spouse, who may feel more strongly about religion than the partner in marriage.

3. Active recruitment to a different religion by a friend, minister, or missionary.

4. An emotional reaction to a life crisis, such as a death or illness in the family, which causes the person affected to seek support in a different religion..

5. Intellectual exploration of atheism or other religions through education, reading or attending services of other denominations.

If one is a member of a dominant religion with friends and neighbors of the same faith, the religious views of one's parents are reinforced by the similar religious views of ones peers, and one is likely to marry within the church. If one is brought up by atheists, however, it is less likely one will attend a Sunday School or have the parents' beliefs reinforced by peers. (In fact, the young atheist is apt to be jeered at or even physically harmed by his or her peers.) The atheist also has a smaller pool of potential spouses to choose among and is thus likely to marry a theist rather than a fellow atheist. Therefore, the first two factors mentioned above are less likely to be determinant for an atheist than for a member of one of the dominant religions. As for the third factor, proselytizing, a change of religion through recruitment is more often from atheist to a theist faith than the reverse. The fourth factor, emotional need, is also more likely to move one away from atheism than toward it.

Therefore, a growth in the number of atheists or even providing a continuing supply to replace those dying off will depend largely on the fifth factor—self-motivation through information acquired in formal education, books, and lectures. Many of the prominent atheists discussed in this book, such as Ingersoll and Darrow, came to atheism through this route.

In the longer term, the increasing number of scientists in America and the acceptance of the scientific method for deciding causes of natural phenomena may boost the prospects of atheism. Religion has already retreated on many scientific questions. Galileo's view that the earth revolves around the sun is now accepted by the Catholic church which persecuted him. Although a minority of right-wing Christians still believe that the Biblical story of creation should be accepted literally, most Christians and Jews now accept Darwin's theory of natural selection as an explanation for evolutionary change of species. With the progress of science, such fields as atomic physics and cosmology lie well outside of traditional religious concerns.

On the other hand, an increasing number of scientists, particularly astrophysicists, have concluded that there could have been a cause for the Big Bang that started the universe we live in. For instance, the Harvard biologist E.O. Wilson wrote in 1998, "On religion I lean toward deism, but consider its proof largely a problem in astrophysics. The existence of a God who created the universe (as envisioned by deism) is possible, and the question may eventually be settled, perhaps by forms of material evidence not yet imagined."[1] There even is a World Union of Deists, headquartered in St. Petersburg, Florida, with their own Web page. They are probably worth `watching.

Recent surveys of scientists seem to show that E.O. Wilson's views are shared by many scientists. In answer to the question: Do you believe in "a God in intellectual and effective communication with man ... to whom one may pray in expectation of receiving an answer"?, sixty percent of the scientists responding said that they did <u>not</u> so believe. Among the 1,800 elite scientists belonging to the National Academy of Science, disbelief exceeded 90 percent, with the figure rising to 95 percent for NAS biologists. It may also be significant that in a similar survey of elite scientists in 1933, the percentage of elite scientists who were nonbelievers was only 80 percent.[2]

Steven Weinberg, a Nobel Prize winner for his work on the theory of particles and fields, has written recently, "One of the great achievements of science has been, if not to make it impossible for intelligent people to be religious, then at least to make it possible for them not to be religious."[3]

It is now generally recognized that education in mathematics and science should be emphasized to prepare our young people for life in a society dominated by technical devices. Scientific education inevitably involves training in scientific methods and rational thinking. Those students who continue their scientific careers may well develop the same religious views as the majority of members of the National Academy of Science mentioned above.

Thus, to the extent that science and scientists become increasingly important in America in the twenty-first century, the dominant religions may face new challenges to their authority. The "village atheist" may no longer be an oddity but rather a figure of respect in a community that has become scientifically literate.

APPENDIX A

AMERICAN BUDDHISTS

All of the atheists, agnostics, and deists, from the Greek Epicureans and Stoics to the American humanists mentioned in this book have been members of minority groups who denied the legitamacy of the belief in the gods or the God of the majority religion. For the Greeks, the intellectual revolt was against the cults of Zeus and Athena; for the French, the disagreement was with Catholicism; for the English, the struggle was against the dominant Church of England; and for the Americans, the fight was against all of the numerous Protestant sects. In contrast, in many parts of Asia, Buddhism is the religion of the majority of the people. Further, its atheism is almost incidental to a completely different set of religious beliefs from the Western religions. Nevertheless, these Buddhists are both atheists and American, and so deserve to be included in this book.

The man known as Buddha, which is a title meaning "Enlightened One," started out life as Siddhartha Gautama and is often known by either of those names or as Sakyamuni, "sage of the Sakya clan." He was born in 560 B.C.in northern India, the son of a chieftain whose family enjoyed relative luxury. Although he was married and had a young son, he decided at age twenty-nine to leave his family and seek a cure for human suffering. After six years of wandering as a beggar, he eventually achieved enlightenment (*bodhi*) while sitting and meditating under the bo tree, the tree of wisdom. Thereafter known as Buddha, he cut off his hair and founded a religious order, Sangha, which first admitted only monks but later included nuns. He preached up and down the Ganges River and died at age 80 near his birthplace. Buddha taught both that human beings have no eternal souls and that there is no cosmic God. He also taught that existence in itself is evil and that one should free oneself from all desire in order to reach a state called nirvana. He apparently based his atheism on the existence of evil and suffering, which he found incompatible with a supreme being.[1]

The teachings of Buddha reached the United States in 1844 thanks to Henry David Thoreau[2]. As we noted in the chapter on the transcendentalists, both Emerson and Thoreau were fascinated by the Eastern religions. Thoreau read a translation of a Buddhist text titled *White Lotus of the Good Law* by the French orientalist Eugene Bournouf. Thoreau then translated this from French to English and published it with commentary in the January 1844 issue of *The Dial*, the transcendentalist magazine edited by Margaret Fuller. In his commentary, Thoreau wrote:

> It does not appear that the Buddha laid any claim himself to miraculous power. In fact, in one of his discourses, occur these remarkable words. A king urged him to confound his adversaries by the exhibition of that superhuman force, which is made to reduce incredulity to silence; "O king!," replied the Buddha, "I do not teach the law to my disciples by saying to them, Go work miracles before the Brahmins and the masters of houses whom you meet, but I teach them in this wise, Live, O holy one by concealing your good works and by exposing your sins." This profound humility, this entire renunciation is the characteristic trait of primitive Buddhism, and was one of the most powerful instruments in its success with the people.[3]

Thirty years later, Felix Adler, the founder of Ethical Culture, also became interested in Buddhism. He wrote an article for *The Atlantic Monthly* titled "A Prophet of the People," which said of Buddha

> The sanctity of the Vedic bible he denied; the immortality of the soul he feared and sought to abrogate, and of the existence of a creator in our sense, he was more than

doubtful....Because of the manifold sweetness which distills from his works and teaching, he will ever be counted in the number of those whom the heart of humanity cherishes as its most loving if they be not its most wise benefactors.[4]

Adler, however, found Buddha too "passive and indifferent to the concerns of the people." Since Adler himself was a social activist, this passivity did not appeal to him.

Both Thoreau and Adler represent the Western, Caucasian view of Buddhism. From the days of Thoreau on, there have existed concurrently two groups of Buddhists in America—the Caucasian students and converts, and the Asian immigrants and their descendants, for whom Buddhism was their native religion. This separation has continued into the twentieth century, with relatively little intercourse between the two branches.

In what is now the United States, the Asian branch of Buddhism probably began in the islands of Hawaii, where a Buddhist sect known as Pure Land Buddhism established a temple around 1839. In the following decade, Chinese immigrants to San Francisco established the Kong Chow and Tien-hou Buddhist temples in that city.[5]

As immigrants from Asia continued to arrive on our shores, they brought the various Buddhist sects with them. There are at least eight major schools of Buddhism, of which Theravada probably is the oldest, as well as many more minor sects.In the Theravada sect, since there is no belief in God, worship services are in a sense only paying respects to a valued teacher. Theravada Buddhism emphasized the individual, who seeksto accumulate good *karma* by performing good acts. The Mahayana sect, on the other hand, substitutes compassion and altruism for the individual striving of Theravada. Other sects include the Pure Land sect mentioned above, and Zen, which is based on a discipline of meditation. Both Zen and Pure Land (referring to a

Pure Land paradise located in the west) and Zen sects are popular in Japan.[6]

Thus, the immigrant Buddhists in America were split not only into various sects but were also divided by whether their ethnic roots were Chinese or Japanese. The Japanese immigrants came over starting in the 1890s, about fifty years after the Chinese. Unlike the Chinese, the Japanese sent Buddhist missionaries to America to support their Buddhist emigrants. These missionaries established Young Men's Buddhist Association (YMBA) groups in imitation of the Christian YMCA and Jewish YMHA organizations. By 1906 there were twelve Pure Land Buddhist temples with Japanese-speaking congregations in California, Washington, and Oregon.[7]

Although the majority of American Buddhists are probably descended from Asian immigrants, over the years a significant number of Caucasians have joined the Buddhist faith. During the late nineteenth and early twentieth centuries, many Americans were influenced by a book titled *The Light of Asia*, written by the British author Edwin Arnold (1832-1904). This book gave a sympathetic account in free verse of the life of Buddha compared with the life of Jesus, It received a number of favorable reviews, including one by the American poet Oliver Wendell Holmes in the *International Review*. It went through eighty American editions and sold more than 500,000 copies. Andrew Carnegie reported that *The Light of Asia* gave him "greater delight than any similar poetical work I had recently read."[8]

Interest in Buddhism was not confined to the East and West coasts. In 1893 the World's Parliament of Religions was held in Chicago along with the Columbian Exhibition, and there were several well-attended Buddhist lectures. Branches of the Maha Bodhi Society, an international Buddhist organization, were established early in the twentieth century in Chicago, Boston, New York, and San Francisco primarily for Caucasian Buddhists.[9]

This interest in Buddhism began to worry the main-line

Christian churches The Reverend Henry M. King, pastor of the First Baptist Church of Providence, Rhode Island, preached a sermon in 1895 saying, "It may be well to take a fresh and, if we can, impartial review of Buddhism...and to inquire seriously—Shall we all become Buddhists?"[10] His fears, however, were not warranted. According to Professor Thomas Tweed (1844-1912), whose book *The American Encounter with Buddhism*, provided the material for much of this chapter, it was not Buddhism's atheism or failure to believe in the immortal soul that impeded its spread in America. Rather it was the Buddhist faith's basic lack of optimism and programs for social action that made it unattractive to most Americans.[11]

Nevertheless, Buddhism is alive and well in America today. Thanks to the Society for the Promotion of Buddhism based in Tokyo, some 2,500 hotels in the United States now carry *The Teaching of Buddha* as well as the Christian *Bible*.[12] In New York City, the former Young Women's Christian Association building on East 15th Street was recently converted into a Buddhist temple.[13]

The directory for the Buddhist Churches of America, lists some sixty churches and temples spread throughout the country. On the other hand, there are undoubtedly many more temples than sixty, probably in sects not represented by this association. The *Statistical Abstract* for 1999 lists 2,445,000 Buddhists in North America. This is approximately ten times the number of Unitarian Universalists.

GLOSSARY

Agnosticism: The view that the ultimate reality of God is unknown and probably unknowable.

Arianism: A heresy that states that the Son is not of the same substance as the Father.

Arminianism: A set of beliefs that rejects predestination and maintains the possibility of universal salvation; similar to Universalism.

Atheism: Disbelief in, or denial of, the existence of God.

Buddhism: A religion based on the teachings of Gautama Buddha, who lived in India about 500 B.C.

Colporteur: One who peddles religious books.

Deism: A belief that God, after creating the universe, never interferes with natural laws.

Epicureanism: A philosophy stemming from Epicurus, who believed that an imperturbable calm was the highest good and that the goal of life should be pleasure, with intellectual pleasure superior to others.

Ethical Culture: A movement founded in America in the late nineteenth century that believes ethics and morality can be based on humanist rather than theological principles.

Eucharist: A Christian ceremony in which bread and wine are partaken in memory of the death of Jesus, also known as communion.

Humanism: A set of beliefs centered on human interests, rejecting all supernatural phenomena, and stressing each

149

individual's dignity and worth.

Infidel: An unbeliever with respect to a particular religion, such as Christianity or Islam.

Pantheism: A doctrine that equates God with the natural laws of the universe.

Socinianism : A doctrine promulgated by the Italian theologian Socinius that rejects the Trinity; similar to Unitarianism.

Stoicism: A philosophy stemming from Zeno of Citrium, who believed that a wise man should be submissive to natural law, free from passion, and indifferent to pleasure and pain.

Transcendentalism: A nineteenth century New England movement based on a belief in the essential unity of all creation, the spark of divinity in all humans, and the supremacy of insight over logic.

Unitarianism: The belief that the deity exists only in one person.

Universalism: Originally a doctrine similar to Arminianism that all men will eventually be saved; now merged with Unitarianism.

NOTES AND SOURCES

INTRODUCTION

1. *The New York Times*, February 27, 1993, p.9.
2. Bureau of the Census, U.S. Department of Commerce, *Statistical Abstract of the United States 1999*, Washington, DC: U.S. Government Printing Office, 1999, Table No. 1348, p.831.
3. Fred Hoyle, "The Universe: Past and Present Reflections," *Engineering & Science*, November 1981, p.12. In the article, Hoyle concludes, "A common sense interpretation of the facts suggests that a superintellect has monkeyed with physics, as well as with chemistry and biology, and that there are no blind forces worth speaking about in nature. The numbers one calculates from the facts seem to me so over-whelming as to put this conclusion almost beyond question.."
4. Timothy Ferris, *The Whole Shebang*, New York: Simon & Schuster, 1997, p.323, note 10.
5. Edward O. Wilson, "The Biological Basis of Morality," *The Atlantic Monthly,* April 1988, p.54.

CHAPTER I: GREEK AND ROMAN ROOOTS
1. Cyril Bailey, *The Greek Atomists and Epicurus*, New York: Russell and Russell, 1964, pp.109-110.
2. Werner Jaeger, *The Theology of the Early Greek Philosophers*, translated by Edward Robinson, Oxford: Clarendon Press, 1947, p.180.
3. Bertrand Russell, *A History of Western Philosophy*, New York: Simon and Schuster, 1945, p.66.
4. Jaeger, p.162.
5. Alban Dewes Winspear, *The Genesis of Plato's Thought,* New York: Dryden Press, 1940, p.150.
6. Russell, p.72.
7. Bailey, p.112.

8. James Thrower, *A Short History of Western Atheism*, London: Pemberton Books, 1971, p.32.

9. Bailey, p.112.

10. Russell, p.243.

11. Letter to William Short, October 31, 1819. In *The Writings of Thomas Jefferson,* eds. A.A. Lipscomb and A.E. Bergh, Washington: Thomas Jefferson Memorial, Vol.XV, p.219.

12. Russell, p.247.

13. David McClellan, *Karl Marx: His Life and Thought*, New York: Harper & Row, 1973, pp.34-38.

14. Karl Marx, *Early Writings,* T.B. Bottomore, ed., "Contribution to the critique of Hegel's Philosophy of Right," New York: McGraw-Hill, 1964, pp.43-44.

15. Cyril Bailey, *Lucretius*, from the Proceedings of the British Academy, Volume XXXV, London: Geoffrey Cambridge Amen House, 1949, p.4.

16. Ibid, pp.8-9.

17. Lucretius, *De Rerum Natura, (Of the Nature of Things),* Book II, line 1090, translated by H.A.J. Munro. In the series Great Books of the Western World, Chicago: Encyclopedia Britannica, 1952.

18. Bailey, *Lucretius*, p.11.

19. Lucretius, Book II, line 1074.

20. Russell, p.251.

21. Thrower, p.35.

22. Epictetus, *Discourses,* tr. by George Long, in the series *Great Books of the Western World*, Chicago: Encyclopedia Britannica, 1952, Vol. 12, p.101.

23. Ibid., Book II, Chapter 8, p.146.

24. Marcus Aurelius, *Meditations,* tr. by George Long, Roslyn, NY: Walter J. Black, 1945, Vol.IV, #23., p.37.,

25. Ibid., Vol.V., #3, p.45.

26. Ibid., Vol.XII, #32, p.132

CHAPTER II: ENGLISH AND FRENCH ROOTS.

1. George T. Buckley, *Atheism in the English Renaissance*, New York: Russell & Russell, 1965, p.31.

2. Ibid, p.42.

3. *Thomas Jefferson's Library: A Catalog with the Entries in His Own Order*, eds. James Gilbreath and Douglas L. Wilson, Washington: Library of Congress, 1989,
in Chapter 24, "Politics."

4. David B. Parke, *The Epic of Unitarianism,* Boston: Starr King Press, 1977, p.24.

5. Buckley, p.57. Buckley's citation is from Stowe, *Annals of England*, 1615, p.695.

6. Ibid., p.58.

7. Sir Leslie Stephen, *Hobbes*, New York: Macmillan. 1904, pp.3-9.

8. Ibid., p.184.

9.Arnold A. Rogow, *Thomas Hobbes: Radical in the Service of Reaction*, New York, W.W. Norton, 1986, p.170.

10. Ibid., p.164.

11. Stephen, p.44.

12. Rogow, p.236.

13. William McIntosh Merrill, *From Statesman to Philosopher: A Study in Bolingbroke's Deism*, New York: Philosophical Library, 1949, p.5.

14. Ibid., p.9.

15. Merrill, p.146-147.

16. Norman L. Torrey, *Voltaire and the English Deists*, New Haven: Yale University Press, 1930, p.149.

17. Will and Ariel Durant, *The Age of Voltaire*, New York: Simon and Schuster, 1965, p.123.

18. James Boswell, *Life of Samuel Johnson,* Oxford: Oxford Press, 1933, Vol.1, p.178.

19. Herbert M. Morais, *Deism in Eighteenth Century America,* New York: Russell & Russell, 1960, p.43.

20. Durant, .pp.140-143.

21. David Hume, *A Treatise of Human Nature,* ed. L.A. Selby-Bigge, Oxford: Clarendon Press, 1978, p.252.

22. David Hume, *An Enquiry Concerning Human Understanding,* ed. Eric Steinberg, Indianapolis: Hackett, 1977, p.78.

23. J.C.A. Gaskin, *Hume's Philosophy of Religion*, London: Macmillan, 1978, p.187.

24. David Hume, *Dialogues Concerning Natural Religion,* ed. Henry D. Aiken, New York: Hafner, 1963, pp.59-60.

25. Hume, *Treatise,* p.94.

26. Hume, *Dialogues*, pp.78-79

27. Nicholas Phillipson, *Hume,* New York, St. Martin's Press, 1989, p.10.

28. Durant, p.696.

29. Gaskin, p.173.

30. Joseph J. Ellis, *American Sphinx: The Character of Thomas Jefferson*, New York: Alfred A. Knopf, 1997, p.98.

31. Durant, p.161.

32. Ibid., p.160.

33. A.J. Ayer, *Voltaire*, New York: Random House, 1986, pp.2-8.

34. Durant, p.132.

35. Ibid., p.726.

36. Ellis, p.77.

37. Ayer, p.34

38. Norman L. Torrey, *The Spirit of Voltaire,* New York: Columbia University Press, 1938, p.230.

39. In Bartlett's *Familiar Quotations, Thirteenth edition*, New York: Little, Brown, 1955, p.325. The citation is *Epitre à l'Auteur du Livre des Trois Imposteurs*, Nov. 10, 1770.

40. Lester G. Crocker, *The Embattled Philosopher: Life of Denis Diderot,* New York: The Free Press, 1954, p.17.

41. Durant, p.624.

42. P.N. Furbank, *Diderot: A Critical Biography,* New York: Alfred A Knopf, 1992, p.25.

43. John Hope Mason, *The Irresistible Diderot*, London: Quartet Books, 1982, pp.33-42.

44. Durant, pp.645-47.

45. Ibid., p.649.

46. Furbank, p.300.

47. Crocker, p.309-310.

48. Durant, p.661. The citation by the Durants is to Diderot's *Oeuvres*, p.220.

49.Arthur M. Wilson, *Diderot: The Testing Years: 1713-1759*, New York: Oxford University Press, 1957, p.8

CHAPTER III: ATHEISM AND DEISM IN THE NEW REPUBLIC.

1. Norman Cousins, *In God We Trust*, New York: Harper. 1958. P.117.
2. William Sterne Randall, *Thomas Jefferson: A Life*, New York: Henry Holt, 1993, p.10.
3. Ibid., p.22.
4. Thomas Jefferson, *Autobiography*, eds. Adrienne Koch and William Peden, New York: Modern Library, 1944, p.4.
5. Gary Wills, *Inventing America: Jefferson's Declaration of Independence*, New York: Doubleday, 1978, pp.175-76.
6. Randall, p.40.
7. Letter to Robert Skipworth, August 3, 1771, *The Papers of Thomas Jefferson*, Julien P. Boyd, ed., Princeton: Princeton University Press, 1950-, Vol.I, p.90.
8. This and other references to the contents of Jefferson's library are mainly based on *Thomas Jefferson's Library: A Catalog with the Entries in His Own Order*, Washington:, Library of Congress, 1977. Jefferson devised his own system for classifying his books under forty-four headings. Bolingbroke, Hume, Diderot, and Voltaire are listed in Chapter 16, "Moral Philosophy," While Machiavelli is in Chapter 24, "Politics," and Lucretius in Chapter 36, "Didactic."
9. Letter to William Short, October 31, 1819, *Writings*, Vol.XV, pp.219-224.
10. Randall, pp.85-86.
11. Charles B. Sanford, *Thomas Jefferson and His Library*, Hamden, CT: Archon Books, 1977, pp.128-133.
12. Randall, p.48.
13. Noble E. Cunningham, Jr., *In Pursuit of Reason: The Life of Thomas Jefferson*, Baton Rouge: Louisiana State University Press, 1987, pp.15-16.
14. Ibid., p.38.
15. Randall, pp.276-278.

16. Benjamin Franklin, *Autobiography,* Mount Vernon, NY: The Peter Pauper Press, 1967, p.12. This abridged version of Franklin's autobiography published by the Peter Pauper Press is a beautiful little book charmingly illustrated.

17. Ibid., p.23.

18. Benjamin Franklin, *Autobiography,* New York: Vintage Books, The Library of America Edition, 1990, p.55. This quotation, unfortunately, does not appear in the Peter Pauper abridged version of the *Autobiography.*

19. Ibid., pp.78-79.

20. Carl Van Doren, *Benjamin Franklin,* New York: Viking Press, 1938, p.132.

21. Herbert M. Morais, *Deism in Eighteenth Century America,* New York: Russell and Russell, 1960, p.42.

22. Ibid., p.655.

23. Ibid., p.391.

24. Albert Henry Smyth, *The Writings of Benjamin Franklin*, New York: Macmillan, 1905, Vol. VI, p.248.

25. Ibid., Vol.VIII, p.462.

26. Howard Fast, *The Selected Work of Thomas Paine*, New York: Modern Library, 1943, Introduction, p.viii-xi.

27.Cousins, p.390-391.

28.John Keane, *Tom Paine: A Political Life,* Boston: Little, Brown, 1995, p.113.

29. Anne Holt, *A Life of Joseph Priestley,* London: Oxford University Press, 1931, pp.7-20.

30. Durant, p.526.

31. Ibid, p.528.

32. Holt, p.138.

33. Van Doren, p.521.

34. Letter from John Adams to Abigail Adams, March 13, 1796, in *Selected Writings of John and John Quincy Adams,* eds. Adrienne Koch and William Peden, New York: Alfred A Knopf, 1946, p.137.

35. Holt, pp.203-204.

36. Ibid, p.140.

37. Letter from Franklin to Ezra Stiles, March 9, 1790. In *Life of Benjamin Franklin*, ed. John Bigelow, Philadelphia: Lippincott, 1905, Vol.III, pp.457-459.

38. Morais, p.66.

39. John Adams, *Diary and Autobiography of John Adams*, ed. L.H. Butterfield, New York: Athenaeum, 1961, Vol.3, p.262.

40. Catherine Drinker Bowen, *John Adams and the American Revolution*, Boston: Little, Brown, 1949, p.133.

41. Morais, p.62.

42. Conrad Wright, *The Beginnings of Unitarianism in America*, Boston: Starr King, 1955, pp.146-147.

43. Adams *Diary*, Vol.3, p.263.

44. Morais, p.70(footnote).

45. Bowen, p.133.

46. Ibid., p.144.

47. Van Doren, p.655.

48. *Public Statutes at Large of the United States of America*, ed. Richard Peters, Boston: Little, Brown, 1848, Vol.VIII, p.155.

49. Randall, pp.292-294.

50. Ibid., p.332.

51. Thomas Jefferson, *Notes on Virginia*, in Cousins, pp.123-124

52. Ellis, p.72.

53. Richard B. Morris, *Witnesses at the Creation: Hamilton, Madison, Jay, and the Constitution*, New York: Holt, Rinehart, 1985, p.104.

54. Cousins, p.117.

55. Morris, p.220.

56. Adrienne Koch, *Madison's Address to My Country*, Princeton: Princeton University Press, 1966, p.33.

57. Cousins, pp.393-394.

58. Ellis, p.216.

59. Wright, pp.243-244.

60. Keane, p.472.

61. Letter from John Adams to Benjamin Rush, Jan. 21, 1810, in Koch and Peden, pp.156-157.

62. Ellis, p.259

63. Letter from John Adams to John Taylor (undated), quoted by Cousins, p.108.

64. Letter from Jefferson to Adams, August 22, 1813. *The Adams-Jefferson Letters,* ed. Lester G. Cappon, Chapel Hill: University of North Carolina Press, 1959, Vol.II, p.368.

65. Letter from Adams to Jefferson, June 20, 1815, in *Selected Writings,* p.191.

66. Letter from Madison to Frederick Beasley, November 20, 1825, quoted in Cousins, p.321.

67. Irving Brant, *James Madison,* Indianapolis: Bobs Merrill, 1961, Vol.I, p.277.

68. George Ticknor, *Life, Letters, and Journals,* Boston: J.H. Osgood, 1876, Vol.I, pp.29-30.

69. Edwin S. Gaustad, *Sworn on the Altar of God,* Grand Rapids, MI: Wm. B. Erdmans, 1996, pp.145-146.

70. Cunningham, p.349.

71. John Adams, *A Biography in his Own Words,* ed. James Bishop Peabody, New York: Harper & Row, 1973, p.407.

72. Ethan Allen, *Reason, the Only Oracle of Man,* New York, J.W. & A.J. Matsell, 1836, Introduction.

73. John Pell, *Ethan Allen,* New York, Houghton Mifflin, 1929, p.253.

74. Ellen D. Larned, *History of Windham County, Connecticut,* Privately Published, 1874, vol.ii, p.221.

75. Morais, p.154.

76. G. Adolph Koch, *Republican Religion: The American Revolution and the Cult of Reason,* Gloucester, MA: Peter Smith, 1964, p.57.

77. Ibid, p.58.

78. Morais, p.130.

79. Koch, p.60.

80. Morais, p.132.

81. Ibid., p.133

82. Koch, p.291.

83. Elihu Palmer, *Principles of Nature: or, A Development of the Moral Causes of Happiness and Misery among the Human Species,* New York: G.H. Evans, 1830, p.19.

84. Ibid, p.25.

85. Charles B.Sanford, *Thomas Jefferson and His Library*, Hamden, CT.: Archon Books, 1977, p.121.

86. Theodore Roosevelt, *Gouverneur Morris*, in American Statesmen series, Vol.VIII, Boston: Houghton Mifflin, 1898, p.251.

87. Barry Schwartz, *George Washington: The Making of an American Symbol*, New York: The Free Press, 1987, p.174.

CHAPTER IV: FANNY WRIGHT, ROBERT OWEN, AND THE COMMUNITARIANS

1. Celia Morris Eckhardt, *Fanny Wright: Rebel in America*, Cambridge, MA: Harvard University Press, 1984, p.66.

2. A.J.G. Perkins and Theresa Wolfson, *Frances Wright: Free Enquirer*, New York: Harper & Brothers, 1939, p.116.

3. Eckhardt, p.109.

4. Horace Traubel, *With Walt Whitman in Camden*, New York: Appleton, 1908, Vol.II, p.205.

5. Eckhardt, pp.6-14.

6. Frances Wright, *A Few Days in Athens*, New York: Arno Press, 1972, p.117.

7. Ibid., p.267.

8. Eckhardt, p.40.

9. Frances Wright, *Views of Society and Manners in America*, Paul R. Baker, ed., Cambridge: Harvard University Press, 1963, p.224.

10. Ibid., p.62, 72.

11. John F.C. Harrison, *Quest for the New Moral World: Robert Owen and the Owenites in Britain and America*, New York, Scribner, 1969, pp. 161-163.

12. Robert Owen. *The Life of Robert Owen, Written by Himself,* New York: A.M. Kelley, 1967, in Reprints of Economic Classics Series, Vol.1, p.206-7.

13. B.C. Hutchins, *Robert Owen*, London: The Fabian Society, 1912, p.12.

14. Harrison, p.164.

15. Arthur Leslie Morton, *The Life and Ideas of Robert Owen*, London: Laurence & Wishart, 1962, p.34.

16. Rowland Hill Harvey, *Robert Owen: Social Idealist*, Berkeley: University of California Press, 1949, p.106.

17. Eckhardt, pp.103-104.

18. Ibid, p.106.

19. Ibid., p.109.

20. Wright, *A Few Days in Athens*, p.211.

21. Arthur Bestor, *Backwoods Utopias*, Philadelphia: University of Pennsylvania Press, 2nd edition, 1970, pp.221-222.

22. Ibid., p.169, footnote 30.

23. Perkins and Wolfson, pp.170-171.

24. Eckhardt, pp.152-155.

25. Frances Trollope, *Domestic Manners of the Americans*, Donald Smalley, ed., New York: Knopf, 1949, p.28 footnote.

26. Ibid., p.110,

27. Ibid., Introduction, p.xxxvii.

28. Alexis de Toqueville, *Democracy in America*, New York: Vintage Books, 1945, p.317.

29. Eckhardt, p.211.

30. Trollope, pp.70-71.

31. Ibid., p.70, footnote 7.

32. Eckhardt, p.175.

33. Ibid., p.191.

34. Ibid., p.199

35. Harrison, p.165.

36. Bestor, p.237.

37. Eckhardt, p.195.

38. Ibid., p.232

CHAPTER V: EMERSON, THOREAU, AND OTHER NEW ENGLAND TRANSCENDENTALISTS.

1. Paul F. Boller, Jr., *American Transcendentalism*, New York: Putnam, 1974, Introduction, p.xx.

2. Gay Wilson Allen, *Waldo Emerson*, New York: Viking Press, 1981, p.39.

3. Ibid., p.58.

4. Ibid., p.73.

5. Samuel Eliot Morison, *Three Centuries of Harvard,* Cambridge: Harvard University Press, 1936, pp.241-244.

6. Allen, p.139.

7. Russell, p.292.

8. Allen, pp.184-185.

9. *The Journals and Miscellaneous Papers of Ralph Waldo Emerson,* eds. William H. Gibson, Alfred R. Ferguson, and Merrell R. Davis, Cambridge: Harvard University Press, 1961, Vol.II, p.3.

10. Ralph Waldo Emerson, *Works*, Four Volumes in One, New York: Tudor Publishing, "Worship", Vol.III, p.158.

11. Walter Harding, *Emerson's Library*, Charlottesville: University of Virginia Press, 1967

12. Warren Staebler, *Ralph Waldo Emerson*, New York: Twayne, 1973, p.92.

13. Allen, p.193.

14. Ibid., p.245.

15. *Emerson's Nature: Origin, Growth, Meaning*, edited by Merton M. Sealts, Jr. and Alfred R. Ferguson, Carbondale, IL: Southern Illinois University Press, 1969, p.8,

16. Ibid., p.8.

17. Ibid., pp.129-130.

18. Ibid., p.85.

19. Joan von Mehren, *Minerva and the Muse: A Life of Margaret Fuller,* Amherst: University of Massachusetts Press, 1994, p.12.

20. Ibid., p.30.

21. Robert D. Richardson, Jr., *Emerson: The Mind on Fire*, Berkeley: University of California Press, 1995, p.241.

22. Allen, p.317.

23. Ibid., p.321.

24. Robert D. Richardson, Jr., *Thoreau: A Life of the Mind*, Berkeley: University of California Press, 1986, p.12.

25. Allen, p.312,

26. Richardson, *Thoreau,* p.38.

27. Ibid., p.71.

28. Ibid., p.103.

29. *The Portable Thoreau,* Carl Bode, ed. New York: Viking Press, 1947, pp.34-35.

30. Allen, p.426.

31. Henry David Thoreau, *Walden, or Life in the Woods,* New York: The Heritage Press, 1939, pp.95-97.

32. *The Portable Thoreau,* p.131.

33. Ibid., p.122.

34. Richardson, *Thoreau,* p.206, and Allen, p.637.

35. Ralph Waldo Emerson, *Selected Writings,* William H. Gilman, *ed.* New York: New American Library, p.471.

36. Henry Steele Commager, *Theodore Parker,* Boston: Little, Brown, 1936, chapters I and II.

37. Richardson, *Emerson,* p.248.

38. Commager, p.46.

39. Ibid., p.45.Quoted from Parker's essay "Thoughts on Labor" in the second issue of *The Dial.*

40. Ibid. p.75.

41. Ibid., pp.88-89.

42. Ibid., pp.132-133.

43. Richardson, *Emerson,* p.405.

44. John White Chadwick, *Theodore Parker: Preacher and Reformer,* Boston: Houghton, Mifflin, 1901, pp.261-263.

45. Richardson, *Emerson,,* p.510.

46. Allen, p.588.

47. Richardson, *Thoreau, p.372.*

48. Ibid., p.389.

49. Allen, p.615.

50. *Selected Writings,* p.476-477.

CHAPTER VI: COLONEL ROBERT INGERSOLL AND OTHER INFIDELS

1. C.H. Cramer, *Royal Bob: The Life of Robert G. Ingersoll,* Indianapolis: The Bobs-Merrill Company, 1952, pp.10-20.

2. Orvin Larson, *American Infidel: Robert G. Ingersoll,* New York" Citadel Press, 1982, pp.26-27.

3. Herman E. Kitterredge, *Ingersoll, A Biographical Appreciation,* New York: Dresden Publishing Company, 1911, p.38.

4. Cramer, p.37.

5. Isaac Newton Baker, *An Intimate View of Robert G.* Ingersoll, New York: C.P. Farrell, 1910, p.55.

6. Ibid., p.27.

7. Robert G. Ingersoll, *Works*, Vol. IV, ed. Clinton B. Farrell, New York: Dresden Publishing, 1902, "Why I Am an Agnostic" p.45.

8. Larson, pp.51-52.

9. *The New York Times*, July 22, 1899, p.3.

10. Cramer, pp.52-54.

11. Larson, p.96.

12. *Cincinnati Enquirer,* June 16, 1876.

13. *New York Times*, Sept. 12, 1876, p.1.

14. Ibid., Sept. 19, p.1.

15. James Turner, *Without God, Without Creed: The Origins of Unbelief in America*, Baltimore: Johns Hopkins University Press, 1985, pp.266-269.

16. Larson, p.129

17. *Daily Nonpareil,* Council Bluffs, Iowa, April 22, 1877, quoted in Larson, p.131.

18. Ibid., pp.155-156

19. Robert Ingersoll, *On the Gods and Other Essays,* Buffalo: Prometheus Books, 1990, pp.54-55.

20. Ibid., pp.100-101.

21. Ibid., pp.170-171.

22. Sidney Warren, *American Freethought, 1860-1914*, New York: Gordian Press, 1966, p.96.

23. Ingersoll, "Why I Am an Agnostic," op.cit.

24. Larson, pp.178-179.

25. Lawrence D. Goodheart, *Abolitionist, Actuary, Atheist: Elizur Wright and the Reform Impulse,* Kent, Ohio: Kent State University Press, 1990, p.23.

26. Ibid., pp.28-32.

27. Ingersoll, *Works*, Vol.XII, pp.409-410.

28. Goodheart, p.184.

29. Ibid., p.186.

30. De Robigne Mortimer Bennett, *The World's Sages, Infidels, and Thinkers,* New York: The Truth Seeker Company, 1876,

pp.1060-1074. Bennett included an autobiographical essay as the last biography of this book.

31. Bennett, *Anthony Comstock, His Career of Cruelty and Crime,* pamphlet extracted from *The Champions of the Church,* pp.1062-1063, New York: Da Capo Press, 1971. The pamphlet retains the page numbers of the larger work from which it was extracted.

32. Heywood Broun and Margaret Leech, *Anthony Comstock,* London: Wishart, 1928, pp.189-197.

33. *Truth Seeker,* Vol.6, Sept. 27, 1879, pp.614-620.

34. Cramer, p.178.

35. Larson, p.279.

36. Cramer, pp.236-238.

37. Larson, pp.252-253.

38. Ibid., p.257.

39. Ibid., p.270.

40. *The New York Times,* July 22, 1899, p.3.

41. Warren, p.175.

CHAPTER VII: THE LAST OF THE ATHEIST ORATORS: CLARENCE DARROW

1. Clarence Darrow, *The Story of my Life,* New York: Scribner's, 1932, p.381

2. Larson, pp.278-279.

3. Darrow, pp.10-14.

4. Ibid., pp.29-30.

5. Kevin Tierney: *Darrow: A Biography,* New York: Thomas Y. Crowell, 1979, pp.42-45.

6. Darrow pp.44-49.

7. Irving Stone, *Clarence Darrow for the Defense,* Garden City, NY: Doubleday, Doran, 1941, pp.41-43.

8. Nick Salvatore, *Eugene Debs: Citizen and Socialist,* Urbana: University of Illinois Press, 1982, p.10.

9. Ibid., p.62, 103-104.

10. Darrow, pp.61-62.

11. Ibid., p.58.

12. Ibid,, p.423.

13. Salvatore, p.150.

14. Darrow, p.68.

15. Stone, p.431.

16. Tierney, p.355.

17. Charles Darwin, *Life and Letters*, edited by his son, Francis Darwin, New York: Basic Books, 1959, Vol.I, p.282.

18. Charles Darwin, *The Descent of Man*, New York: Hurst, 1874, pp.109-110. The 1874 book, from which this quotation was taken, is the second edition, which expands on a similar paragraph in the first edition.

19. Stone, p.429.

20. *The New York Times*, July 9, 1925, p.1.

21. Tierney, p.363.

22. *The New York Times,* July 16, 1925, p.2.

23. Ibid., July 18, 1925, p.1; July 21, 1925, p.2.

24. Stone, p.457.

25. *The New York Times,* July 21, 1925, p.1.

26. Ibid., July 22, 1925, p.2.

27. Ibid.

28. Darrow, p.274.

29. Tierney, p.372.

30. Ibid., p.399.

31. Darrow, p.387.

32. Ibid., p.404.

33. Ibid., p.413.

CHAPTER VIII: UNITARIANS AND UNIVERSALISTS
THE FREE RELIGIOUS ASSOCIATIOIN

1. Membership information from Unitarian Universalist Association, 25 Beacon Street, Boston, Massachusetts.

2. *1996 Statistical Abstract of the United States*, Washington: U.S. Department of Commerce, Table 1324, p.826.

3. Conrad Wright, *The Liberal Christians: Essays on American Unitarian History*, Boston: Beacon Press, 1970, pp.110-112.

4. David B. Parke, *The Epic of Unitarianism*, Boston: Starr King Press, 1977, p.60.

5. Ibid., pp.55-56.

6. Wright, pp.113-114.

7. See Chapter V, p.XXX.

8. Ibid., p.XXX.

9. Henry Steele Commager, *Theodore Parker,* Boston: Little, Brown, 1966, pp.74-75.

10. Andrew Delbanco, *William Ellery Channing: An Essay on the Liberal Spirit in America,* Cambridge: Harvard University Press, 1981, p.113.

11. Parke, p.118.

12. Daniel Walker Howe, "At Morning Blest and Golden Brown,", in *A Stream of Light: A Short History of American Unitarianism,* ed. Conrad Wright, Boston: Skinner House, 1989, pp.58-59.

13. Ibid., p.60.

14. Parke, p.121.

15. Sidney Warren, *American Freethought, 1860-1914,* New York: Gordian Press, 1966, pp.99-101.

16. Ibid., pp.104-105.

17. Stow Persons, *Free Religion, an American Faith,* Boston, Beacon Press, 1963, p.25.

18. Warren, p.102.

19. Parke, pp.126-127.

20. Ibid., p.137.

21. Wilson, Edwin H., *The Genesis of a Humanist Manifesto,* Amherst, NY: Humanist Press, 1995, p.8.

22. Parke, p.140.

23. Warren R. Ross, "The Marginalized Majority", in November/December 1997 issue of *World* magazine, the journal of the Unitarian Universalist Association, p.16..

24. The Rev. Brian Eslinger, the Rev. Sarah Oelberg, and the Rev. Victoria Safford, "Why I Am a Humanist," *World* magazine, November/December 1997, pp.17-19.

25. Gregory Wolfe, ed., *The New Religious Humanists: A Reader,* New York: The Free Press, 1997.

26. Carol R. Morris, "It Was Noontime Here..." in *A Stream of Light: A Short History of American Unitarianism,* ed, Conrad Wright, Boston: Skinner House Books, 1959, pp.151-154.

27. Warren R. Ross, "The Marginalized Majority," *World* magazine, November/December, 1997, p.14.

28. Tom Stiles, "Diverse Theologies, Common Values," *World* magazine, May/June 1998, p.38.

29. *World* magazine, July/August, 1998, p.8.

30. *The Humanist* magazine, May/June 1998, p.34.

31. Ed Doerr, "Humanism and Unitarian Universalism." in *The Humanist*, March/April 1988, p.37

CHAPTER IX: ETHICAL CULTURE.

1. Robert S. Guttchen, *Felix Adler,* New York: Twayne, 1974, pp.17-22.

2. Howard B. Radest, *Felix* Adler: *An Ethical Culture*, New York: Peter Lang, 1998, pp.9-10.

3. Guttchen, p.26.

4. Howard B. Radest, *Toward Common Ground,* New York: Frederick Ungar, 1969, pp.17-19.

5. Ibid., p.29.

6. *The New York Times*, April 4, 1878.

7. Guttchen, p.24.

8. Stow Persons, *Free Religion, an American Faith,* Boston: Beacon Press, 1963, p.96.

9. Radest, *Toward Common Ground,* pp.41-44.

10. Ibid., p.49

11. Ibid., pp.62-65.

12. Ibid., pp.146-147.

13. Ibid., pp.110-115.

14. Ibid., pp.265-267.

15. Edward L. Ericson, *The Humanist Way*, New York: CONTINUUM, 1988, pp.8-10.

16. Radest, p.238.

17. www.aeu.org, "How to Find a Real Ethical Society: Member Societies, American Ethical Union."

18. Membership figure from headquarters of the American Ethical Union, 2 West 64th St., New York City.

CHAPTER X: THE AMERICAN HUMANIST ASSOCIATION

1. Corliss Lamont, *The Philosophy of Humanism*, Eighth Edition (Revised), Amherst, NY: Humanist Press, 1997, p.3.
2. Edward L. Ericson, *The Humanist Way: An Introduction to Ethical Humanist Religion,* New York: CONTINUUM, 1998, Introduction pp.xiii-xiv.
3. Edwin H. Wilson, *The Genesis of a Humanist Manifesto,* Amherst, NY: Humanist Press, 1995, pp.16-18.
4. Ibid., pp.20-21.
5. Ibid., pp.26-33.
6. The final text of *A Humanist Manifesto* may be found on pp.96-99 of Wilson's book and in the May/June 1933 issue of *The New Humanist.*
7. Ibid., p.100.
8. Howard B. Radest, *Toward Common Ground: The Story of the Ethical Societies of the United States,* New York: Frederick Ungar, 1969, p.269.
9. Wilson, pp.106-108.
10. Ibid, p.152-3.
11. Ibid., p.154-5.
12. Radest, p.324.
13. Wilson, p.16.
14. *Humanist Manifesto II* is available on the Internet at www.humanist.net under Humanist Documents and Statements. It is also reprinted on pp.290-300 of Corliss Lamont's book *The Philosophy of Humanism* mentioned at the start of this chapter.
15. Paul Kurtz, "Beyond Humanist Manifesto II," *The Humanist,* September/October 1998, p.27.
16. Wilson, pp.190-191.
17. Advertisement in *The Humanist,* September/October, 1998, p.46.
18. Ibid., pp.33-39.
19. Www.humanist.net, AHA Chapter Information as of September 1998.
20. Circulation of *The Humanist* from national office of the American Humanist Association in Amherst, NY. Circulation of *World* from article in the May/June 1998 issue, p.36.

CHAPTER XI: AMERICAN ATHEISTS (ORGANIZED AND UNORGANIZED)

1. Madelyn Murray O'Hair, *An Atheist Epic*, Austin TX: American Atheist Press, 1989, pp.ix-xii.

2. Institute for First Amendment Studies, *Freedom Writer,* March, 1989.

3. O'Hair, p.40.

4. Ibid. p.293.

5. Gerald Tholen, "The Way It Was," *American Atheist,* June, 1983, p.7. Also reprinted in *An Atheist Epic*, pp.296-297.

6. William J. Murray, *My Life Without God,* Nashville: T. Nelson, 1982.

7. *The New York Times*, April 21, 1996, Section 1, p.34.

8. Sam Howe Verhovec, *The New York Times,* December 22, 1996, Section 1, p.14.

9. *The New York Times,* March 28, 1999, Section 4, p.2.

10. Marshall Sella, "Godless and Proud of It," *The New York Times*, December 7, 1977, Section 6, p.103.

11. Ibid.

CHAPTER XII: THE SLOW GROWTH OF AMERICAN DEISM AND ATHEISM

1. Edwin S. Gaustad, *Sworn on the Altar of God,* Grand Rapids, Michigan: Wm. B. Erdmans, 1996, pp.145-146.

2. Bureau of the Census, U.S. Department of Commerce, *Statistical Abstract of the United States 1999*, Washington, D.C.: U.S. Government Printing Office, 1999, Table 1348, p.831.

3. Paul K. Conkin, *American Originals: Homemade Varieties of Christianity*, Chapel Hill, NC, University of North Carolina Press, 1997

4. Michael Schermer and Frank Sulloway, "Why People Believe in God." *The Humanist*, November\December, 1999, pp.20-26

5. Malcolm Dean, *The Astrology Game: The Truth about Astrology*, New York, Beaufort Books, 1980, p.24.

6. Michael Schermer, *Why People Believe in Weird Things*, New York, W.H. Freeman, 1997, p.276.

7. E.J. Kahn, Jr., *Harvard: Through Change and Through Storm,* New York, W.W. Norton, 1969, p.252.

8. George Wilson Pierson, *Yale: The University College, 1921-1987,* New Haven, Yale University Press, p.221.

CHAPTER XIII: THE FUTURE OF AMERICAN DEISM AND ATHEISM

1. Edward O. Wilson, "The Biological Basis of Morality," *The Atlantic Monthly*, April, 1998, p.54.

2. Edward J. Larson and Larry Witham, "Scientists and Religion in America," *Scientific American,* September 1999, pp.88-93.

3. Steven Weinberg, "A Designer Universe?," *The New York Review of Books*, October 21, 1999, p.48.

APPENDIX A: AMERICAN BUDDHISTS

1. *The Encyclopedia of Philosophy*, Paul Edwards, ed., New York: Macmillan & The Free Press, Vol.I, pp.416-417.

2. Thomas A. Tweed, *The American Encounter with Buddhism, 1844-1912: Victorian Culture and the Limits of Dissent,* Bloomington: Indiana University Press, 1992, Introduction, p.xix.

3. Henry David Thoreau, "The Preaching of Buddha," *The Dial,* Vol.IV, No.3, January, 1844, pp.391-392.

4. Felix Adler, "A Prophet of the People," *The Atlantic Monthly*, Vol. 37, June 1876, pp.683-689.

5. Website buddhist@tiac.net, "Frequently Asked Questions", p.9.

6. *Encyclopedia of Philosophy*, pp.417-418.

7. Tweed, p.36.

8. Ibid, pp.29, 44, 46.

9. Ibid, p.27.

10. Ibid., p.26.

11. Ibid, p.254.

12. Edwin McDowell, "Bible Now Shares Hotel Rooms with Some Other Good Books," *The New York Times,* December 26, 1995, Sect. A, p.14.

13. Christopher Gray, "Streetscapes/The 'Y' at 7 East 15th Street," *The New York Times*, September 18, 1994, Sect. 9, p.7.

BIBLIOGRAPHY

Adams, John and John Quincy, *Selected Writings of John and John Quincy Adams*, eds. William Koch and William Peden, New York: Alfred A. Knopf, 1946.

Adams, John, *Diary and Autobiography of John Adams*, ed. L.H. Butterfield, New York: Athenaeum, 1961.

Adams, John, and Thomas Jefferson,, *The Adams-Jefferson Letters*, ed. Lester G. Cappon, Chapel Hill: University of North Carolina Press, 1959.

Adams, John, *A Biography in His Own Words*, ed. James Bishop Peabody, New York: Harper & Row, 1973.

Allen, Ethnan, *Reason, the Only Oracle of Man*, New York: J.W. and A.J. Matsell, 1836.

Allen, Gay Wilson, *Waldo Emerson*, New York: Viking Press, 1991.

Antoninus, Marcus Aurelius, *Meditations*, Translated by George Long, Roslyn, NY:Walter J. Black, 1945.

Ayer, A.J., *Voltaire*, New York: Random House, 1986.

Bailey, Cyril, *The Greek Atomists and Epicurus*, New York: Russell & Russell, 1964.

———, *Lucretius*, Proceedings of the British Academy, Vol. XXXV, London: Geoffrey Cambridge Amen House, 1949.

Baker, Isaac Newton, *An Intimate View of Robert G. Ingersoll*, New York: C.P. Farrell, 1910.

Bennett, De Robigne Mortimer, *The World's Sages, Infidels, and Thinkers*, New York: The Truth Seeker Company, 1876.

——— , *Anthony Comstock, His Career of Cruelty and Crime*, New York: De Capo Press, 1971.

Bestor, Arthur, *Backwoods Utopias*, Philadelphia: University of Pennsylvania Press, 1970.

Bigelow, John, *Life of Benjamin Franklin*, Philadelphia: Lippincott, 1905.

Boller, Paul F., Jr., *American Transcendentalism*, New York: Putnam, 1984.

Boswell, James, *Life of Samuel Johnson*, Oxford: Oxford Press, 1933.

ATHEISTS, AGNOSTICS, AND DEISTS IN AMERICA

Bowen, Catherine Drinker, *John Adams and the American Revolution,* Boston, Little, Brown, 1949.

Brant, Irving, *James Madison,* Indianapolis:Bobs Merrill, 1961.

Broun, Heywood and Leech, Margaret, *Anthony Comstock,* London: Wishart, 1928.

Buckley, George T., *Atheism in the English Renaissance,* New York: Russell & Russell, 1965.

Chadwick, John White, *Theodore Parker: Preacher and Reformer,* Boston: Houghton, Mifflin, 1901.

Commager, Henry Steele, *Theodore Parker,* Boston: Little, Brown, 1936.

Conkin, Paul K. , *American Originals: Homemade Varieties of Christianity,* Chapel Hill: Univ. of North Carolina Press, 1997.

Cousins, Norman, *In God We Trust,* New York: Harper, 1958.

Cramer, C.H., *Royal Bob: The Life of Robert G. Ingersoll,* Indianapolis: Bobs-Merrill, 1952.

Crocker, Lester G., *The Embattled Philosopher: Life of Denis Diderot,* New York: The Free Press, 1954.

Cunningham, Noble E., Jr., *In Pursuit of Reason: The Life of Thomas Jefferson,* Baton Rouge: Louisiana State University Press, 1987.

Darrow, Clarence, *The Story of My Life,* New York: Scribner's, 1932.

Darwin, Charles, *The Descent of Man,* New York: Hurst, 1874.

————, *Life and Letters,* ed. Francis Darwin, New York: Basic Books, 1959.

Dean, Malcolm: *The Astrology Game: The Truth about Astrology,* New York: Beaufort Books, 1980.

Delbanco, Andrew, *William Ellery Channing: An Essay on the Liberal Spirit in America,* Cambridge: Harvard University Press, 1981.

Durant, Will and Ariel, *The Age of Voltaire,* New York: Simon & Schuster, 1965.

Eckhardt, Celia Morris, *Fanny Wright: Rebel in America,* Cambridge: Harvard University Press, 1984.

Ellis, Joseph J., *American Sphinx: The Character of Thomas Jefferson,* New York: Alfred A. Knopf, 1997.

Emerson, Ralph Waldo, *Works,* Four Volumes in One, New York: Tudor Publishing.

———— , *Selected Writings,* ed.William H. Gilman, New York: New

BIBLIOGRAPHY

American Library.

———, *The Journals and Miscellaneous Papers of Ralph Waldo Emerson,* eds. William H. Gibson, Alfred R. Ferguson, and Merrell R. Davis Cambridge: Harvard University Press, 1961.

———, *Emerson's "Nature": Origin, Growth, Meaning,* eds. Merton M. Sealts, Jr. and Alfred R. Ferguson, Carbondale, Illinois: Southern Illinois University Press, 1969.

Epictetus, *Discourses,* Translated by George Long, Chicago: Encyclope dia Brittanica, 1952.

Ericson, Edward L. *The Humanist Way: An Introduction to Ethical Humanist Religion,* New York: CONTINUUM, 1998.

Fairbank, P.N., *Diderot: A Critical Biography,* New York: Alfred A. Knopf, 1992.

Franklin, Benjamin, *The Writings of Benjamin Franklin,* ed. Albert Henry, New York: Macmillan, 1905.

———, *Autobiography,* New York: Vintage Books, 1950.

Gaskin, J.C.A., *Hume's Philosophy of Religion,* London: Macmillan, 1978.

Gaustad, Edwin S., *Sworn on the Altar of God,* Grand Rapids: William B. Erdmans. 1996.

Goodheart, Lawrence D., *Abolitioist, Actuary, Atheist: Elizur Wright and the Reform Impulse,* Kent, Ohio: Kent State University Press, 1990.

Guttchen, Robert S., *Felix Adler,* New York: Twayne, 1974.

Harding, Walter, *Emerson's Library,* Charlottesville: University of Virginia Press, 1967.

Harrison, John F.C. *Quest for he New Moral World: Robert Owen and the Owenites in Britain and America,* New York: Scribner, 1969.

Harvey, Rowland Hill, *Robert Owen: Social Idealist,* Berkeley: University of California Press, 1949.

Holt, Anne, *A Life of Joseph Priestly,* London: Oxford University Press, 1931

Hume, David, *Dialogues Concerning Natural Religion,* ed. Henry D. Aiken, New York: Hafner, 1963.

———, *An Enquiry Concerning Human Understanding,* ed. Eric Steinberg, Indianapolis: Hackett, 1977.

ATHEISTS, AGNOSTICS, AND DEISTS IN AMERICA

————, *A Treatise of Human Nature*, ed. L.A. Selby-Bigge, Oxford, Clarendon Press, 1978.

Hutchins, B.C., *Robert Owen*, London: The Fabian Society, 1912.

Ingersoll, Robert G., *On the Gods and Other Essays*, Buffalo: Prometheus Books, 1990.

————, *Works*, Clinton B. Farrell, ed., New York: Dresden Publishing, 1902.

Jaeger, Werner, *The Theology of the Early Greek Philosophers*, Oxford: Clarendon Press, 1947.

Jefferson, Thomas, *The Papers of Thomas Jefferson*, ed. Julien P. Boyd, Princeton: Princeton University Press, 1950.

————, *The Writings of Thomas Jefferson*, eds. A.A. Lipscomb and A.E. Bergh, Washington:Thomas Jefferson Memorial, 1904.

————, *Autobiography*, eds. Adrienne Koch and William Peden, New York: Modern Library, 1944.

————, *Thomas Jefferson's Library: A Catalog with Entries in his Own Order*, eds. James Gilbraith and Douglas L. Wilson, Washington: Library of Congress, 1989.

Kahn, E.J., Jr., *Harvard: Through Change and Through Storm*, New York: W.W. Norton, 1969.

Keane, John, *Tom Paine: A Political Life*, Boston: Little, Brown, 1995.

Kitterrredge, Herman E., *Ingersoll, A Biographical Appreciation*, New York: Dresden Publishing, 1911.

Koch, Adrienne, *Madison's Address to My Country*, Princeton: Princeton University Press, 1966.

Koch, G. Adolph, *Republican Religion: The American Revolution and the Cult of Reason*, Gloucester, Massachusetts: Peter Smith, 1964..

Lamont, Corliss, *The Philosophy of Humanism*, Amherst, NY: Humanist Press, 1997.

Larned, Ellen D,, *History of Windham County, Connecticut*, Privately Published, 1874

Larson, Edward J. and Witham, Larry, "Scientists and Religion in America," *Scientific American*, September, 1999, pp.88-93.

BIBLIOGRAPHY

Larson, Orvin, *American Infidel: Robert G. Ingersoll*, New York, C.P.
Farrell, 1910.
Lucretius, *De Rerum Natura (Of the Nature of Things)*, Trans. by
H.A.J. Munro, Chicago: Encyclopedia Brittanica, 1952.

Marx, Karl, *Early Writings*, ed. T.B. Bottomore, New York: McGraw-
Hill, 1964.
McClellan, David, *Karl Marx: His Life and Thought*, New York:
Harper & Row, 1973.
Mehren, Joan von, *Minerva and the Muse: A Life of Margaret   Fuller*,
Amherst: University of Massachusetts Press, 1994.
Merrill, William McIntosh, *From Statesman to Philosopher: A Study
in Bolingbroke's Deism*, New York: Philosophical Library,
1949.
Morais, Herbert M., *Deism in Eighteenth Century America*, New York:
Russell & Russell, 1960.
Morison, Samuel Eliot, *Three Centuries of Harvard*, Cambridge: Har-
vard University Press, 1936.
Morris, Richard B., *Witnesses at the Creation: Hamilton, Madison,
Jay, and the Constitution*, New York: Holt, Rinehart, 1985.
Morton, Arthur Leslie, *The Life and Ideas of Robert Owen*, London:
Laurence and Wishart, 1962.
Murray, William J., *My Life Without God*, Nashville: T. Nelson,
1982.

O'Hair, Madelyn Murray, *An Atheist Epic*, Austin, TX: American
Atheist Press, 1989.
Owen, Robert, *The Life of Robert Owen, Written by Himself*, New
York: A.M. Kelley, 1967.

Paine, Thomas. *The Selected Work of Thomas Pains*, ed. Howard
Fast, New York: Modern Library, 1943.
Palmer, Elihu, *Principles of Nature; or, a Development of the Moral
Causes of Happiness and Misery among the Human Species*,
New York: G.H. Evans, 1830.
Parke, David B., *The Epic of Unitarianism*, Boston: Starr King Press,
1977.
Pell, John, *Ethan Allen*, New York: Houghton Mifflin, 1929.
Perkins, A.J.G. and Wolfson, Theresa, *Frances Wright: Free Enquirer*,

New York: Harper Brothers, 1939.

Persons, Stow, *Free Religion, An American Faith*, Boston: Beacon Press, 1963.

Philipson, Nicholas, *Hume,* New York, St. Martin's Press, 1939.

Pierson, George Wilson, *Yale: The University College, 1921-1987*, New Haven: Yale University Press, 1988.

Radest, Howard B.,, *Felix Adler: An Ethical Culture*, New York, Peter Lang: 1998.

————, *Toward Common Ground: The Story of the Ethical Societies of the United States*, New, York: Frederick Ungar, 1969.

Randall, William Sterne, *Thomas Jefferson: A Life*, New York: Henry Holt, 1993.

Richardson, Robert D., Jr., *Emerson: The Mind on Fire*, Berkeley: University of California Press, 1996.

Rogow, Arnold A., *Thomas Hobbes: Radical in the Service of Reaction,* New York: W.W. Norton, 1986.

Rossevelt, Theodore, *Gouverneur Morris*, Boston: Houghton Mifflin, 1898.

Russell, Bertrand, *A History of Western Philosophy*, NewYork: Simon and Schuster, 1945.

Salvatore, Nick, *Eugene Debs: Citizen and Socialist,* Urbana: University of Illinois Press, 1982.

Sanford, Charles B., *Thomas Jefferson and His Library*, Hamden, Connecticut: Archon Books, 1977.

Schermer, Michael, *Why People Believe in Weird Things,*New York: W.H. Freeman, 1997.

Schermer, Michael and Sulloway, Frank, "Why People Believe in God," *The Humanist*, Nov./Dec. 1999.

Schwartz, Barry, *George Washington: The Making of an American Symbol*, New York: The Free Press, 1987.

Staebler, Warren, *Ralph Waldo Emerson,* New York: Twayne, 1973.

Stephen, Leslie, *Hobbes*, New York: Macmillan, 1904.

Stone, Irving, *Clarence Darrow for the Defense,* Garden City, NY: Doubleday, Doran, 1941.

BIBLIOGRAPHY

Thoreau, Henry David, *Walden, or Life in the Woods*, New York: The Heritage Press, 1939.

——, *The Portable Thoreau*, ed. Carl Bode, New York: Viking Press, 1947.

Thrower James, *A Short History of Western Atheism*, London: Pemberton Books, 1971.

Ticknor, George, *Life, Letters, and Journals*, Boston: J.H. Osgood, 1876.

Tierney, Kevin, *Darrow: A Biography*, New York: Thomas Y. Crowell, 1979.

Toquevile, Alexis de, *Democracy in America*, New York: Vintage Books, .1945.

Torrey, Norman L., *Voltaire and the English Deists*, New Haven: Yale University Press, 1930.

Torrey, Norman L., *The Spirit of Voltaire*, New York, Columbia University Press, 1938.

Traubel, Horace, *Walt Whitman in Camden*, New York: Appleton, 1908.

Trollope, Frances, *Domestic Manners of the Americans*, ed. Donald Smalley, New York: Knopf, 1949.

Turner, James, *Without God, Without Creed: The Origins of Unbelief in America*, Baltimore: John Hopkins University Press, 1995.

Tweed, Thomas A., *The American Encounter with Buddhism, 1844-1912: Victorian Culture and the Limits of Dissent*, Bloomington: Indiana University Press, 1992.

Van Doren, Carl, *Benljamin Franklin*, New York: Viking Press, 1938.

Warren, Sidney, *American Freethought, 1860-1914*, New York: Gordian Press, 1966.

Weinberg, Steven, "A Designer Universe?", *The New York Review of Books*, October 21, 1999.

Wills, Gary: *Inventing America: Jefferson's Declaration of Independence*, New York Doubleday, 1978.

Wilson, Arthur M., *Diderot: The Testing Years: 1713-1759*, New York: Oxford University Press, 1957.

Wilson, Edward O., "The Biological Basis of Morality," *The Atlantic Monthly*, April, 1998.

ATHEISTS, AGNOSTICS, AND DEISTS IN AMERICA

Wilson, Edwin H., *The Genesis of a Humanist Manifesto*, Amherst, NY: Humanist Press, 1995.

Winspear, Alban Dewes, *The Genesis of Plato's Thought,*New York: Dryden Press, 1940.

Wolfe, Gregory, ed., *The New Religious Humanists: A Reader*, New York: The Free Press, 1997.

Wright, Conrad, ed., *A Stream of Light: A Short History of American Unitarianism*, Boston: Skinner House, 1989.

———, *The Beginnings of Unitarianism in America*, Boston: Starr King, 1955.

———, *The Liberal Christians: Essays on American Unitarian History*, Boston: Beacon Press, 1970.

Wright, Frances, *Views of Society and Manners in America*, ed. Paul R. Baker, Cambridge: Harvard University Press, 1963.

———, *A Few Days in Athens*, New York: Arno Press, 1972.

INDEX

INDEX

INDEX